The Gen X Series

IMO NSO NCO IEO

International Mathematics Olympiad National Science Olympiad National Cyber Olympiad International English Olympiad

OLYMPIAD SAMPLE PAPERS 8

Useful for Olympiads Conducted at School, National & International Levels

Compiled By
Editorial Board

Strictly According to the Latest Syllabus of Olympiad

V&S PUBLISHERS

Published by:

V&S PUBLISHERS

F-2/16, Ansari road, Daryaganj, New Delhi-110002
☎ 23240026, 23240027 • *Fax:* 011-23240028
Email: info@vspublishers.com • *Website:* www.vspublishers.com

Regional Office : Hyderabad
5-1-707/1, Brij Bhawan (Beside Central Bank of India Lane)
Bank Street, Koti, Hyderabad - 500 095
☎ 040-24737290
E-mail: vspublishershyd@gmail.com

Branch Office : Mumbai
Jaywant Industrial Estate, 1st Floor–108, Tardeo Road
Opposite Sobo Central Mall, Mumbai – 400 034
☎ 022-23510736
E-mail: vspublishersmum@gmail.com

BUY OUR BOOKS FROM: AMAZON FLIPKART

ISBN 978-93-579423-3-1

New Edition

DISCLAIMER

Publisher's Note

The current decade has firmly established V&S Publishers as one of the Leading Publishers of General Trade Mass Appeal Books across popular genres along with Academic Books for School Children. Having been in publishing trade for over 40 years, we understand the need of the hour when it comes to Books. After successfully publishing around 600 titles in the last decade and establishing a pan India network of booksellers & distributors including ecommerce platforms – Amazon, Flipkart etc; we determined after a nation-wide market research in tier 1, 2 and 3 cities that preparatory materials for status-acquiring OLYMPIAD BOOKS is the need of the hour.

And in true spirit, the Olympiad books on Science, Maths, English and Cyber published for classes 1 to 10 was picked by students off the shelf in no time. It acquired the 'Bestseller' image. Encouraged by this huge acceptability of our Olympiad Series among parents, students and booksellers alike, we at V&S Publishers decided to take PREPARATION to the next level by bringing out another handholding masterpiece – Olympiad Sample Papers.

These Sample Papers are the virtual replicas of the actual exam papers.

Yes! These Sample Papers are the virtual replicas of the actual exam papers. Inclusion of two sets each for Science, Maths, English and Cyber subjects from classes 1 to 10 in respective books are believed to be adequate to prepare students mentally for 'live exam conditions.' Anything else would have been 'under-preparation' or over-preparation'

You will hardly be able to differentiate the Sample Papers from the Actual Exam Papers. All this has been made possible by the people who have been in their respective fields for years – coaching and guiding students to succeed in this vital exam.

P.S. While every care has been taken to ensure correctness of content, if you come across any error, howsoever minor, anywhere in the book, do not hesitate to discuss with your teachers while pointing that out to us in no uncertain terms.

We wish you All the Best!

Contents

INTERNATIONAL MATHEMATICS OLYMPIAD (IMO)

1. Mock Test Paper – 1 9
2. Mock Test Paper – 2 15

NATIONAL SCIENCE OLYMPIAD (NSO)

3. Mock Test Paper – 1 23
4. Mock Test Paper – 2 29

NATIONAL CYBER OLYMPIAD (NCO)

5. Mock Test Paper – 1 37
6. Mock Test Paper – 2 43

INTERNATIONAL ENGLISH OLYMPIAD (IEO)

7. Mock Test Paper – 1 49
8. Mock Test Paper – 2 56

HINTS AND SOLUTIONS 62

INTERNATIONAL MATHEMATICS OLYMPIAD (IMO)

Mock Test Paper 1

Total Questions : 50 | Time : 1 Hour

I M O

INTERNATIONAL MATHEMATICS OLYMPIAD

PATTERN AND MARKING SCHEME				
Section	**(1) Logical Reasoning**	**(2) Mathematical Reasoning**	**(3) Everyday Mathematics**	**(4) Achievers Section**
No. of Questions	15	20	10	5
Marks per Questions	1	1	1	3

SYLLABUS

Section – 1 : Verbal and Non-Verbal Reasoning.

Section – 2 : Real Numbers, Polynomials, Pair of Linear Equations in Two Variables, Quadratic Equations, Arithmetic Progressions, Triangles, Coordinate Geometry, Introduction to Trigonometry, Some Applications of Trigonometry, Circles, Constructions, Areas Related to Circles, Surface Areas and Volumes, Statistics, Probability.

Section – 3 : The Syllabus of this section will be based on the syllabus of Mathematical Reasoning and Quantitative Aptitude.

Section – 4 : Higher Order Thinking Questions – Syllabus as per Section – 2.

LOGICAL REASONING

1. Find the term which replace the question mark to complete the given series.
   0, 6, 24, 60, 120, 210, ?
   (A) 412 (B) 336
   (C) 202 (D) 290

2. In a certain code, NOIDA is written as 39658. Following the same rule of coding, what should be the code word for INDIA?
   (A) 35468 (B) 63568
   (C) 23459 (D) 36954

3. A is B's father's nephew. C is B's cousin but not the brother of A. How is C related to A if A has only one uncle?
   (A) Brother
   (B) Aunt
   (C) Sister
   (D) None of these

4. Sameera went to attend a wedding ceremony of her cousin in another city situated 5 km away in the North-East direction of her own city. From there she came to meet her brother-in-law living in another city situated 4 km in the South of her cousin's city. How far away and in which direction is she now from her own city?
   (A) 2 km in the South
   (B) 3 km in the East
   (C) 6 km In the North
   (D) None of these

5. In the given figure, square represents engineers, triangle represents males and circle represents authors. By which letter the males who are both engineers and authors represented ?

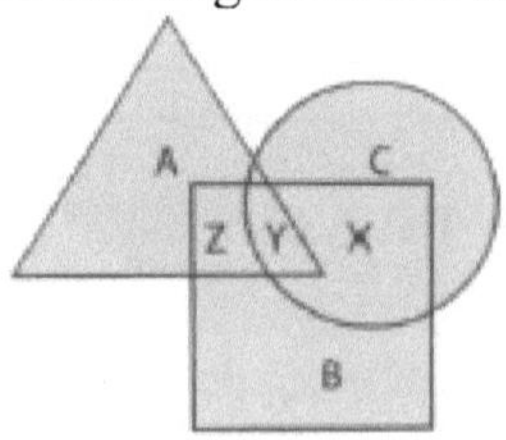

(A) Z (B) Y
(C) B (D) C

6. Arrange the words given below in a meaningful sequence.

i. Puberty ii. Adulthood
iii. Childhood iv. Infant
v. Adolescence

(A) iv, iii, i, v, ii (B) ii, iv, iii, i, v
(C) v, ii, iii, iv, i (D) None of these

7. If a stands for –, b stands for ÷, c stands for + and d stands for ×, then 15 b 3 c 24 a 12 d 2 = ?

(A) 24 (B) 4
(C) 5 (D) $\frac{2}{9}$

8. How many triangles are there in the figure given below?

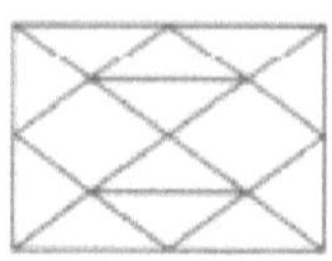

(A) 40 (B) 18
(C) 24 (D) 32

9. Choose the correct mirror image of the figure (X) from the given options as mirror is being placed to the left of the figure.

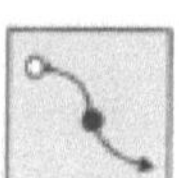
(X)

(A) 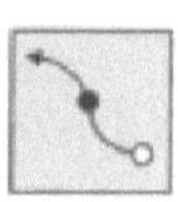 (B) 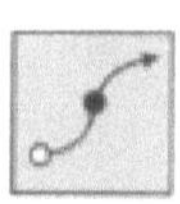

(C) 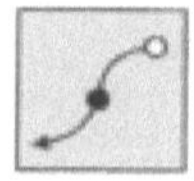 (D) 

10. Select a figure from the options that can replace the question mark(?) in order to complete the given figure matrix.

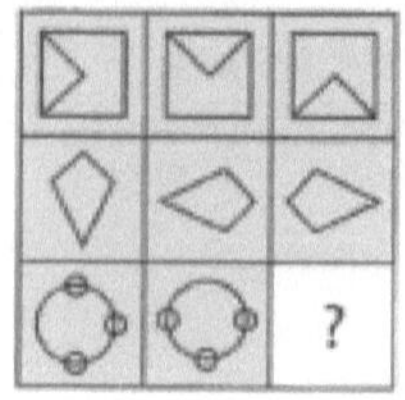

(A) 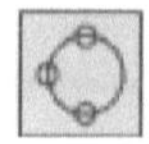 (B) 

(C)  (D) 

11. There are three square sheets of paper marked as X, Y and Z. X and Y show two consecutive folds of the sheet respectively. And the figure Z shows cuts of the folded sheet. Choose the figure that is the unfolded form of the sheet.

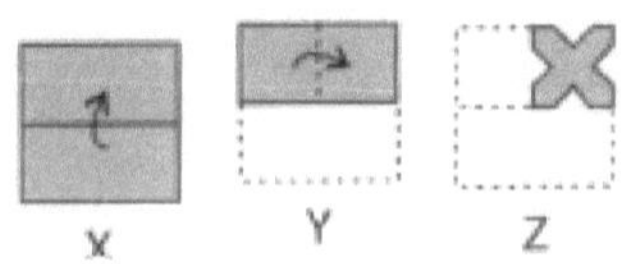

(A)  (B) 

(C)  (D) 

12. Choose the box that is similar to the box formed by folding the given sheet (X) of paper.

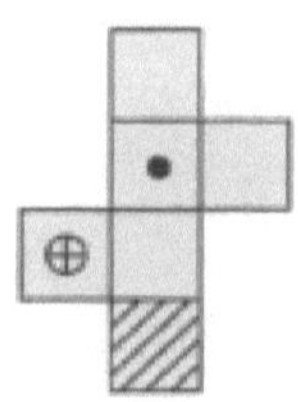
(X)

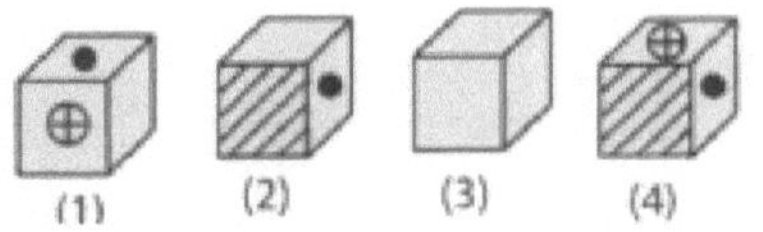

(A) 1 and 4 only
(B) 1 only
(C) 1 and 2 only
(D) 1, 3 and 4 only

13. To establish the same relationship between two pair of terms on either side of '::' choose the correct term that will replace the question mark ?
7 : 49 :: 24 : ?
(A) 137
(B) 421
(C) 576
(D) None of these

14. Select a figure from the options which satisfies the same conditions of placement of the dots as in Fig. (X).

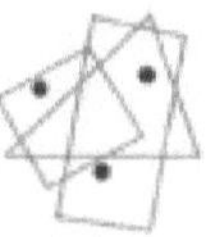

Fig. (X)

(A) 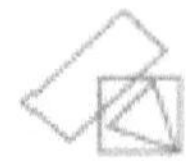
(B) 
(C) 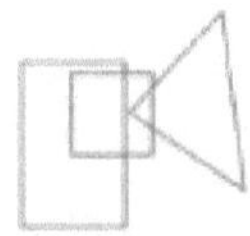
(D) 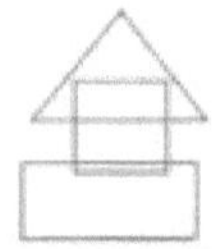

15. Figure X and Y given below shows positions of a dice. When 2 is at the bottom, which number will be at the top?

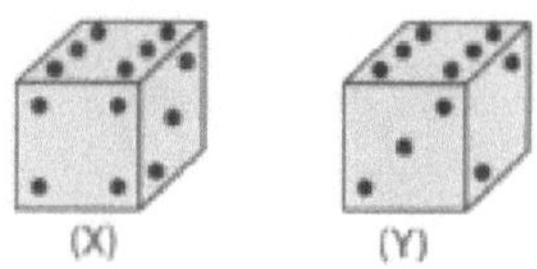

(A) 2
(B) 6
(C) Can't be determined
(D) 4

MATHEMATICAL REASONING

16. Find the multiplicative inverse of $\frac{0}{1}$.
(A) Not defined
(B) 0
(C) 2
(D) –3

17. Which of the following shapes has a vertex.

(A) 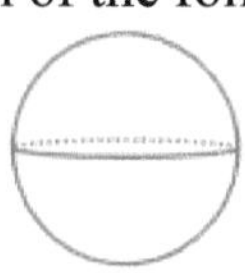
(B) 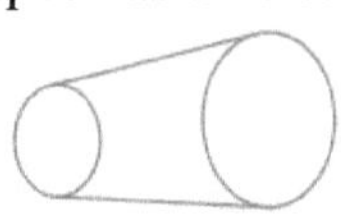
(C) 
(D) 

18. The following pie chart shows the number of candidates from team P, Q, R and S taking part in a football match. If there are 18 candidates from team S, find the number of candidates from team R.

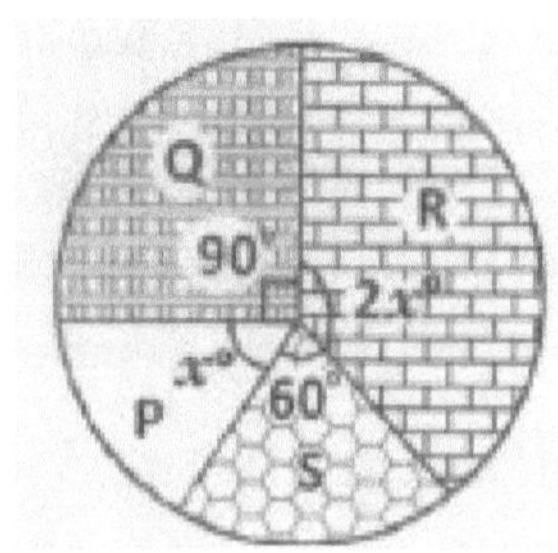

(A) 12 (B) 42
(C) 36 (D) 16

19. If $3^{m-n} = 27$ and $3^{m+n} = 243$, then evaluate the value of m.
(A) 1 (B) 4
(C) 0 (D) 8

20. Akansha has a total of ₹ 300 in coins of denomination ₹ 1, ₹ 2 and ₹5. The number of ₹ 2 coins is 3 times the number of ₹ 5 coins. The total number of coins is 160. How many coins of ₹ 5 denomination she has?

(A) 20 (B) 40
(C) 10 (D) 30

21. The marked price of an article is ₹ 500. The shopkeeper gives a discount of 5% and still makes a profit of 25%. Find the cost price of the article.

(A) ₹ 680 (B) ₹ 380
(C) ₹ 450 (D) None of these

22. Find the number of sides of a polygon if its each interior angle is 108°

(A) 5 (B) 7
(C) 6 (D) 8

23. Akshita's present age is thrice of Shilpa. If Shilpa's age three years ago was x. Then find Akshita's present age.

(A) $3(x-3)$ (B) $3x+3$
(C) $3x-9$ (D) $3(x+3)$

24. If $x+y=17$ and $x^2+y^2=167$, what is the value of xy ?

(A) 61 (B) 128
(C) $15+4\sqrt{114}$ (D) $42+\sqrt{167}$

25. Pipes A and B can fill a tank in 18 minutes and 12 minutes respectively. If both the pipes are opened simultaneously, how long will they take to fill the tank ?

(A) 30 minutes (B) 20 minutes
(C) 10 minutes (D) $7\frac{1}{5}$ minutes

26. If the altitude of an equilateral triangle is $\sqrt{6}$ cm, find its area.

(A) $2\sqrt{3}$ cm^2 (B) $2\sqrt{2}$ cm^2
(C) $6\sqrt{2}$ cm^2 (D) $3\sqrt{3}$ cm^2

27. On a scale map 0.7 cm represents 8.4 km. If the distance between two points on the map is 4.65 cm, what is the actual distance between the points ?

(A) 56 km (B) 55.80 km
(C) 72 km (D) 62.80 km

28. Find the value of x in the given figure?

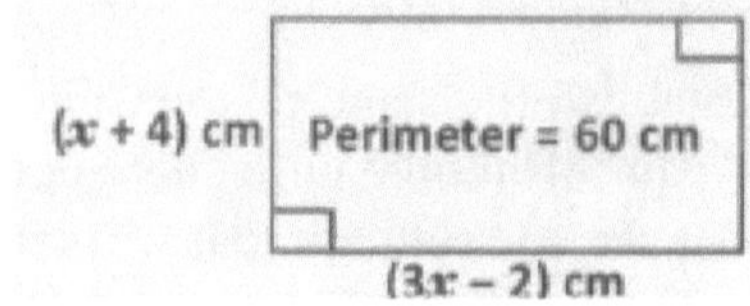

(A) 7 (B) 9
(C) 12 (D) 29

29. What is the usual form of $100a+b+10c$.

(A) *cab* (B) *abc*
(C) *bca* (D) *acb*

30. The compound interest on a certain sum of money for 2 years at 10% per annum is ₹ 420. Find the simple interest on the same sum at the same rate and for the same time.

(A) ₹ 350 (B) ₹ 375
(C) ₹ 380 (D) ₹ 400

31. The ratio of radii of two cylinders having equal volume is 3 : 1. Then, find the ratio of their heights.

(A) 1 : 9
(B) 1 : 3
(C) 3 : 1
(D) $\sqrt{3}:1$

32. Evaluate $\sqrt{248+\sqrt{52+\sqrt{144}}}$.

(A) 24 (B) 26
(C) 16 (D) 13

33. 30 men can reap a field in 17 days. If the field is to be reaped in 10 days, then how many extra men will be required to complete the given task?

(A) 51 (B) 21
(C) 12 (D) None of these

34. Find the value of $(x^2 - y^2)$ if $x = \sqrt{2}$ and $y = \frac{1}{\sqrt{2}}$

(A) 3/2 (B) 1
(C) 0 (D) 4/3

35. When a ball is drawn randomly from a bag which contains 4 red, 6 black and 8 blue balls. Then, find the possible outcomes.

(A) 8 (B) 7
(C) 9 (D) 18

EVERYDAY MATHEMATICS

36. A man walks around a circular track of radius 21 m with a speed of 6 km/hr. If he takes 30 rounds of the track, for how long does he walk?

(A) 26 min and 24 s
(B) 39 min and 36 s
(C) 20 min and 2 s
(D) None of these

37. A committee decided to collect fund for a charity programme as many rupees from each member as is the number of members. If the total collection amounts to ₹ 2209, then find the number of members in the committee.

(A) 107 (B) 37
(C) 47 (D) 53

38. A boat goes downstream and covers the distance between two ports in 3 hours while it covers the same distance in 5 hours when it goes upstream. If the stream flows at 3 km/hr, then find what is the speed of the boat upstream?

(A) 6 km/hr
(B) 9 km/hr
(C) 12 km/hr
(D) 4 km/hr

39. A survey shows a data that 40% of the buyers are interested in buying a particular brand of shampoo. Find the central angle of the sector of the pie chart representing this information.

(A) 110° (B) 120°
(C) 154° (D) 144°

40. A gunny bag contains balls of different colours of which 80 are red, 24 are white and the rest are blue. If the probability of randomly selecting a blue ball is $\frac{1}{5}$, then how many blue balls are there in the bag?

(A) 15 (B) 16
(C) 26 (D) 12

41. Aman purchased a car worth ₹ 300000 and a bike for his brother for ₹ 100000. He sold the car at a profit of 10% and bike at a loss of 20%. What is the net gain or loss?

(A) 1% loss
(B) 2.5% gain
(C) 3.5% gain
(D) 1.5% loss

42. Ananya gets 3 marks for each correct sum and loses 2 marks for each incorrect sum. He does 24 sums and obtains 37 marks. What was the number of correct sums ?

(A) 40 (B) 16
(C) 17 (D) 28

43. Radhika bought an air-conditioner for Rs 15,200 and spent Rs 300 and Rs 500 on its transportation and repair respectively. At what price should she sell it to make a profit of 15%?

(A) ₹ 18400 (B) ₹ 17500
(C) ₹ 20200 (D) None of these

44. In a camp, 600 men had provisions for 180 days. After 40 days, 100 men left the camp. For how many days does the remaining food last?
(A) 150 days
(B) 200 days
(C) 168 days
(D) None of these

45. Rahul covers a particular distance at 56 km/h and completes his journey in 4 hours. If his speed is 64 km/h, then find the time taken to complete the same journey?
(A) $3\frac{1}{2}$ hrs (B) $4\frac{2}{5}$ hrs
(C) $3\frac{3}{4}$ hrs (D) None of these

ACHIEVERS SECTION

46. If $y=\frac{1}{2}$, find the value of $y+\cfrac{1}{1+\cfrac{1}{1+\cfrac{1}{y}}}$.
(A) 1/4 (B) 2/5
(C) 5/4 (D) None of these

47. A rectangular sheet of paper is rolled to form a cylinder along its length. Find the volume of cylinder so formed if the sheet measures 44 cm × 33 cm.
(A) 4560 cm^3 (B) 5082 cm^3
(C) 3600 cm^3 (D) 7280 cm^3

48. Akshay borrows a sum of money which doubles itself in 4 years at compound interest. In how many years will it amount to 8 times itself at the same rate of interest ?
(A) 8 years (B) 12 years
(C) 20 years (D) 42 years

49. If $\sqrt{1+\frac{64}{225}}=1+\frac{x}{15}$, what is the value of '$x$'?
(A) 1 (B) 8
(C) 2 (D) 5

50. If $3^{\left(\frac{y}{2}-2\right)}=9y$, find the value of y.
(A) 5/4 (B) 1/3
(C) –4/3 (D) None of these

Mock Test Paper 2

Total Questions : 50 Time : 1 Hour

I M O

INTERNATIONAL MATHEMATICS OLYMPIAD

PATTERN AND MARKING SCHEME				
Section	**(1) Logical Reasoning**	**(2) Mathematical Reasoning**	**(3) Everyday Mathematics**	**(4) Achievers Section**
No. of Questions	15	20	10	5
Marks per Questions	1	1	1	3

SYLLABUS

Section – 1 : Verbal and Non-Verbal Reasoning.

Section – 2 : Real Numbers, Polynomials, Pair of Linear Equations in Two Variables, Quadratic Equations, Arithmetic Progressions, Triangles, Coordinate Geometry, Introduction to Trigonometry, Some Applications of Trigonometry, Circles, Constructions, Areas Related to Circles, Surface Areas and Volumes, Statistics, Probability.

Section – 3 : The Syllabus of this section will be based on the syllabus of Mathematical Reasoning and Quantitative Aptitude.

Section – 4 : Higher Order Thinking Questions – Syllabus as per Section – 2.

LOGICAL REASONING

1. Identify the pattern followed in given figure and find the missing term which will replace the question mark.

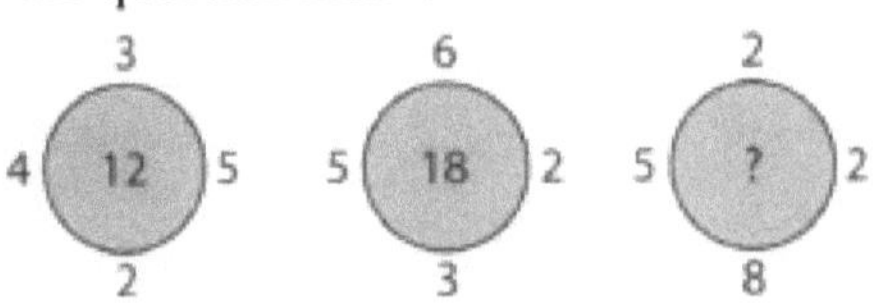

(A) 20 (B) 16
(C) 10 (D) 8

2. Which of the following completes the first pair in the same way as the second pair?

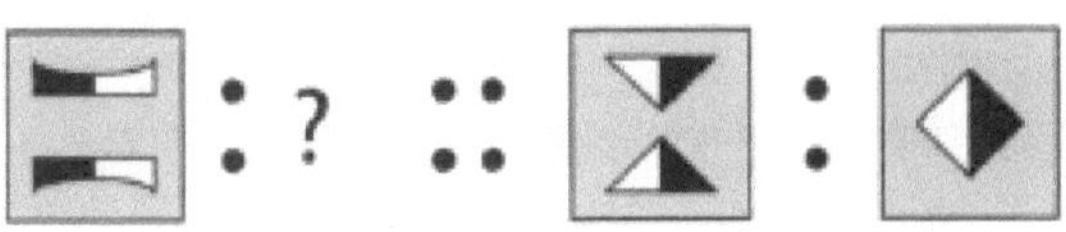

(A)  (B) 

(C)  (D) 

3. If 'sky' is 'star', 'star' is 'cloud', 'cloud' is 'earth', 'earth' is 'tree' and 'tree' is 'book', then where do the birds fly?
(A) Book
(B) Star
(C) Earth
(D) Data insufficient

4. Sajal pointing towards Aanchal, "This girl is the daughter of only child of my father". How is Sajal's wife related to Aanchal ?
(A) Daughter
(B) Mother
(C) Sister
(D) Sister-in-law

5. Arya goes 12 km towards North from a fixed point and then she goes 8 km towards South from there. In the end she goes 3 km towards East. How far and in which direction is she from her starting point?
(A) 4 km, West
(B) 6 km, East
(C) 5 km, North-East
(D) 2 km, East

6. In the Venn- Diagram given below, triangle represents 'boys', rectangle represents 'athletes' and circle represents 'coach'.
Which part of the diagram represents the boys who are athletes but not coach?

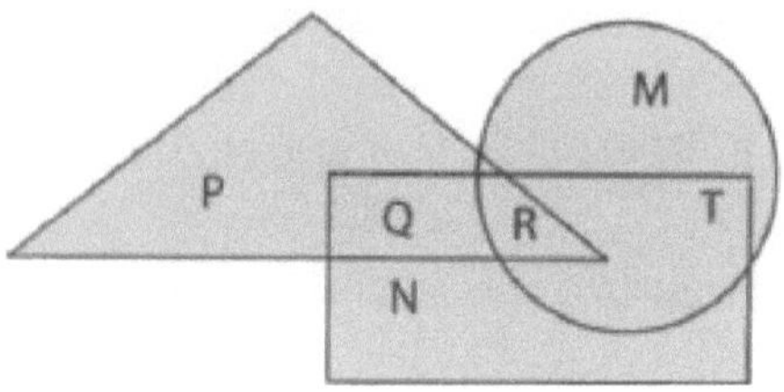

(A) Q (B) M
(C) N (D) R

7. If – denotes ÷, + denotes ×, ÷ denotes –, × denotes +, then which of the following equations is correct?
(A) $36 \times 4 - 12 + 5 + 3 = 420$
(B) $52 \div 4 + 5 \times 8 - 2 = 36$
(C) $36 - 12 \times 6 + 3 + 4 = 60$
(D) $43 \times 7 + 5 + 4 - 8 = 25$

8. In a row of boys, Anshul is 20th from the right end and Sahil is 10th from the left end. When they interchange their positions Anshul becomes 25th from the right end. What is the total number of boys in the row?
(A) 24 (B) 34
(C) 25 (D) 14

9. Count the number of parallelograms in the given figure.

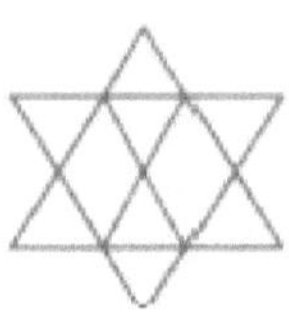

(A) 16 (B) 15
(C) 20 (D) 8

10. Select the one from the options which satisfies the same condition of placement of the dots in the figure (X).

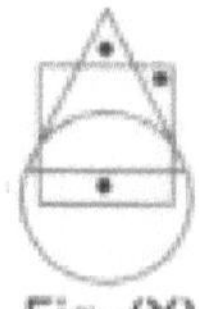

Fig. (X)

(A)  (B) 

(C) 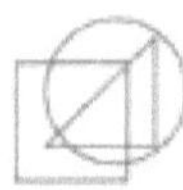 (D) 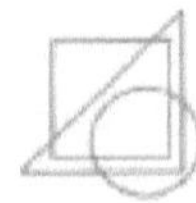

11. Choose the box that is similar to the box formed from the given sheet (X) of paper.

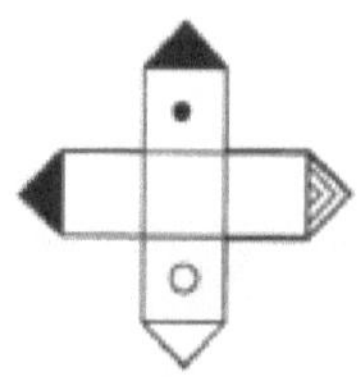

(X)

(A)  (B) 

(C)  (D) 

12. A transparent sheet X with a design and a dotted line on it is given. This sheet X is to be folded along the dotted line. Choose the correct figure from the options, that is similar to the folded form of the sheet X.

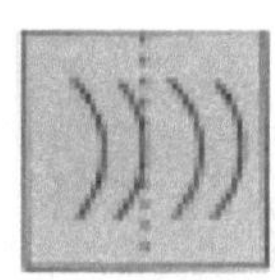

Fig. (X)

(A) 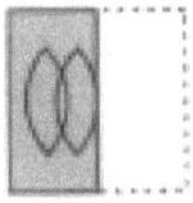 (B) 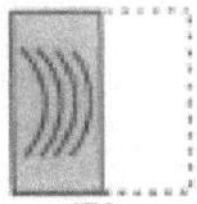

(C) 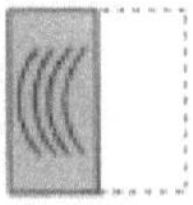 (D) 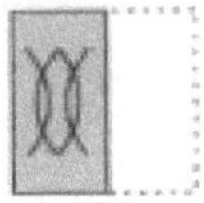

13. Find out the figure from the options given below that completes the figure matrix?

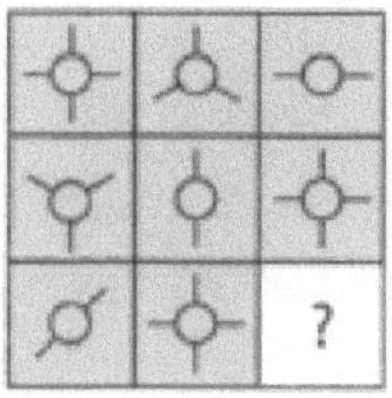

(A)  (B) 

(C)  (D) 

14. Choose the suitable water image of the given figure (X) from options given below.

(X)

(A)  (B) 

(C)  (D) 

15. The figure (X) is exactly embedded in any one of the four options. Identify the correct option.

(X)

(A) 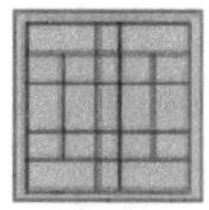 (B) 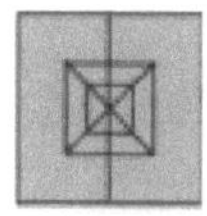

(C)  (D) 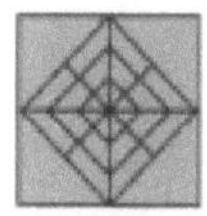

MATHEMATICAL REASONING

16. Find out the coordinates of point Q in the given graph?

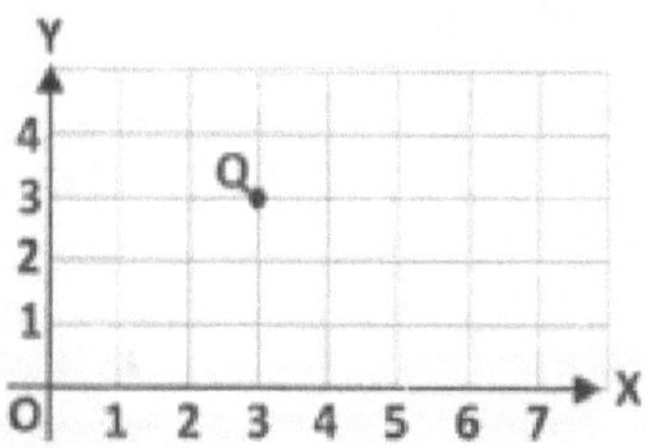

(A) (0, 6) (B) (6, 10)
(C) (3, 3) (D) None of these

17. In a scout camp, there is food provision for 300 cadets for 42 days. If 50 more persons join the camp, for how many days will the provision last?
(A) 56 days (B) 28 days
(C) 36 days (D) 46 days

18. Given that $\sqrt{2401} = 49$, then find the value of $\sqrt{0.2401} + \sqrt{24.01}$
(A) 53.9 (B) 5.39
(C) 0.49 (D) 49.05

19. The parallel sides of a trapezium are 40 cm and 20 cm. If its height being 24 cm, find the area of the trapezium.
(A) 420 cm^2 (B) 720 cm^2
(C) 550 cm^2 (D) 850 cm^2

20. Factorize $p^2 - 17p - 38$
(A) $(p-19)(p+2)$
(B) $(p-19)(p-2)$
(C) $(p+19)(p+2)$
(D) None of these

21. The difference in S.I. and C.I. on a certain sum of money in 2 years at 15% p.a. is ₹144. Find the sum.
(A) ₹ 8000 (B) ₹ 6200
(C) ₹ 6700 (D) ₹ 6400

22. Find the length of one of the diagonals of a rectangle whose sides are 10 cm and 24 cm.
(A) 28 cm (B) 10 cm
(C) 26 cm (D) 3.5 cm

23. Two numbers are in the ratio 3 : 5. If 9 is subtracted from each, the new numbers are in the ratio 12 : 23. Find the smaller number.
(A) 24 (B) 38
(C) 42 (D) 55

24. In a parallelogram ABCD, if AB = $2x + 5$, CD = $y + 1$, AD = $y + 5$ and BC = $3x - 4$, what is the ratio of AB and BC ?
(A) 71 : 21 (B) 12 : 11
(C) 31 : 35 (D) 4 : 7

25. ABCD is a rectangular park and its diagonals meet at O. Find x, if OA = $2x + 4$ and OD = $3x + 1$.

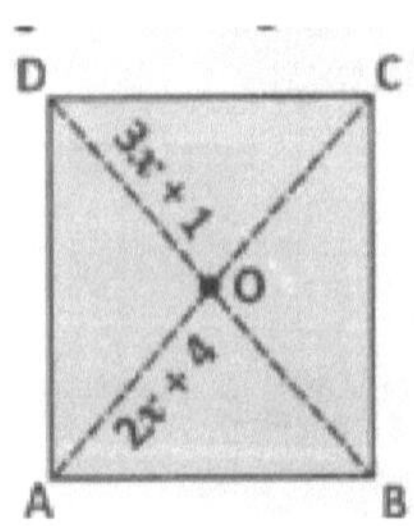

(A) 4 (B) 3
(C) –2 (D) –4

26. Identify the true statement.
(A) The Y-axis is a horizontal line
(B) The point of intersection between the X-axis and Y-axis is called the origin.
(C) The X-axis is a vertical line.
(D) The scale on both the axes must be the same in a Cartesian plane.

27. Find the number of sides of a polygon if each angle of a regular polygon is 135°?
(A) 7
(B) 6
(C) 8
(D) None of these

28. Find the generalized form of a three-digit number xyz.
(A) $x + y + z$
(B) $100x + 10y + z$
(C) $100y + 10x + z$
(D) $100z + 10y + x$

29. If marked price of an article is ₹ 1,200 and the discount is 12%, then find the selling price of the article.
(A) ₹ 1056 (B) ₹ 1424
(C) ₹ 1222 (D) ₹ 1080

30. Find the value of $[15625 \times -(729)]^{\frac{1}{3}}$.
(A) 215 (B) –225
(C) –252 (D) –525

31. If $\frac{5x}{3} - 4 = \frac{2x}{5}$, then find the value of x.
(A) 60/19 (B) 55/19
(C) 32/19 (D) None of these

32. If $N = \sqrt[3]{\sqrt[3]{a^9}}$, then find the value of N?
(A) a^8 (B) a^5
(C) a (D) $\left(a^3\right)^3$

33. Identify the solid that does not have any curved surface?
(A) 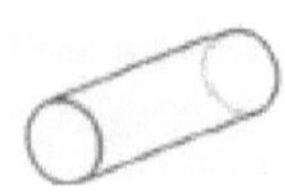 (B) 
(C)  (D) 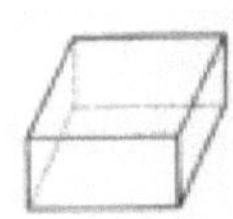

34. Identify the rational number from the options below, which is equivalent to $\frac{-5}{-3}$

(A) $\frac{-35}{15}$ (B) $\frac{25}{15}$

(C) $\frac{-25}{15}$ (D) $\frac{-25}{20}$

35. What is the probability of selecting 'W' from the letters of the word WRITE ?

(A) $\frac{2}{5}$ (B) $\frac{1}{5}$

(C) 1 (D) 0

EVERYDAY MATHEMATICS

36. Two pipes X and Y can fill a tank in 18 minutes and 12 minutes respectively. If both the pipes are opened simultaneously, how long will they take to fill the tank ?

(A) 40 minutes

(B) $7\frac{1}{5}$ minutes

(C) 12 minutes

(D) 16 minutes

37. Maya put some coloured bangles on the table. There were 4 blue, 7 red, 3 yellow and 6 orange bangles in all. Suddenly, a cat jumped on the table and knocked out one bangle on the floor. What is the probability that the bangle on the floor is red?

(A) $\frac{7}{20}$ (B) $\frac{1}{4}$

(C) $\frac{1}{5}$ (D) None of these

38. If a group of 20 persons working together can finish a job in 20 days, find the time taken by a group of 25 persons of the same capacity to finish the job.

(A) 22 days (B) 16 days

(C) 21 days (D) 40 days

39. In a maths project, Meera has to convert a square sheet of paper into a cylinder by rolling it along its side. Find the ratio of the base radius to the side of the square?

(A) $1:2\pi$ (B) $3:2\pi$

(C) $1:3\pi$ (D) $1:4\pi$

40. Roma has a farm house in the shape of a rectangle whose sides are 10 cm and 24 cm. Find the length of one of its diagonal.

(A) 25 cm (B) 26 cm

(C) 2.5 cm (D) 24 cm

41. A class room has a capacity of 2304 seats. If the number of rows is equal to the number of seats in each row, then find the number of seats in each row.

(A) 36

(B) 52

(C) 48

(D) None of these

42. There are 2000 students in a school. The pie chart given below shows the interest of students in different subjects. How many students are interested in Science?

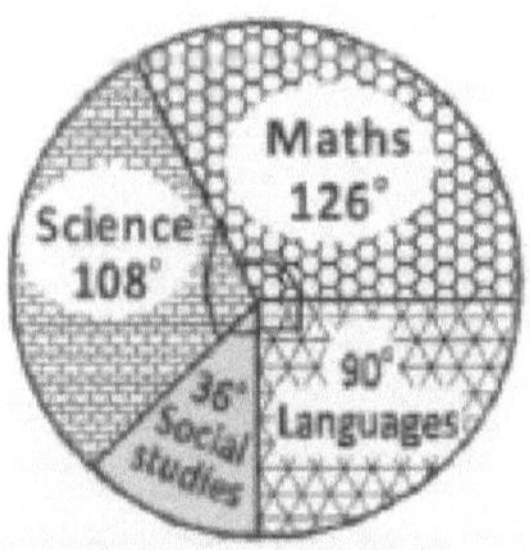

(A) 700 (B) 600

(C) 500 (D) 200

43. Arun sold two houses for ₹ 3,75,890 each. On one he gains 15% but on the other he loses 15%. How much does he gain or lose in the whole transaction ?

(A) 2% loss (B) 4.2% loss

(C) 2.25% loss (D) 4.2% gain

44. The square roots of Radhika's and Kartik's ages have a sum of 7 and a difference of 1. If Radhika is older than Kartik, how old is Radhika ?

(A) 12 years (B) 16 years
(C) 3 years (D) 8 years

45. There are 3 bags of rice. Bag Y weighs thrice as much as bag X and bag Z weighs 4 kg less than bag Y. If bag X weighs 6 kg, how heavy is bag Z?

(A) 20 kg (B) 42 kg
(C) 14 kg (D) 22 kg

ACHIEVERS SECTION

46. If $3x - \frac{1}{3x} = 6$, find the value of $81x^4 + \frac{1}{81x^4}$.

(A) 1250
(B) 1442
(C) 1632
(D) None of these

47. If $3^y = \frac{\sqrt{3}}{9}$, find the value of y.

(A) –3/2 (B) 2/3
(C) –2 (D) 3

48. Evaluate $\sqrt[3]{\sqrt{0.000064}}$

(A) 0.02 (B) 0.2
(C) 2 (D) 0.002

49. The difference between S.I. and C.I. compounded yearly at the rate of 4% in two years period on a certain amount of money is ₹ 1. Find the amount.

(A) ₹ 800
(B) ₹ 625
(C) ₹ 550
(D) ₹ 875

50. A covered wooden box has the inner measures as 115 cm, 75 cm and 35 cm and thickness of wood as 2.5 cm. Find the volume of the wood.

(A) 85, 000 cm^3
(B) 80, 000 cm^3
(C) 82, 125 cm^3
(D) 84, 000 cm^3

NATIONAL SCIENCE OLYMPIAD (NSO)

Mock Test Paper 1

NSO
NATIONAL SCIENCE OLYMPIAD

Total Questions : 50 Time : 1 Hour

PATTERN AND MARKING SCHEME			
Section	**(1) Logical Reasoning**	**(2) Science**	**(3) Achievers Section**
No. of Questions	10	35	5
Marks per Questions	1	1	3

SYLLABUS

Section – 1: Verbal and Non-Verbal Reasoning.

Section – 2: Crop Production and Management, Microorganisms, Synthetic Fibres and Plastics, Metals and Non-metals, Coal and Petroleum, Combustion and Flame, Conservation of Plants and Animals,-Cell, Reproduction and Endocrine System,Force and Pressure, Friction, Sound, Chemical Effects of Electric Current, Some Natural Phenomena, Light, Stars and the Solar System, Pollution of Air and Water.

Section – 3: Higher Order Thinking Questions – Syllabus as per Section – 2.

LOGICAL REASONING

1. Arrange the following words in a meaningful sequence.
   a: Introduction
   b: Arrival
   c: Presentation
   d: Recommendation
   e: Discussion
   (A) b, a, c, e, d (B) d, e, a, b, c
   (C) c, a, d, e, b (D) e, a, b, d, c

2. Identify the Venn diagram which shows the best relationship between Animals, Cow and Tiger.
   (A) 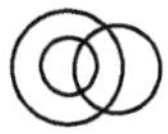 (B) 
   (C)  (D) 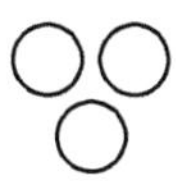

3. Read the statement and conclusion carefully and identify which of the conclusions correctly follows the meaning of the statement.
   Statement: Some elephants are parrots. Some parrots are tigers.
   Conclusions:
   C1: Some elephants are tigers.
   C2: All parrots are tigers.
   (A) Only C1 follows
   (B) Only C2 follows
   (C) Both C1 and C2 follows
   (D) Neither C1 nor C2 follows

4. What can replace the question mark?
   Battery : Terminals :: Magnet : ?
   (A) Terminals (B) Poles
   (C) Charge (D) Magnetism

5. Find the odd one out.
   (A) Explosion (B) Hurricane
   (C) Earthquake (D) Cyclone

6. What can replace the question mark in the given image to complete the series?

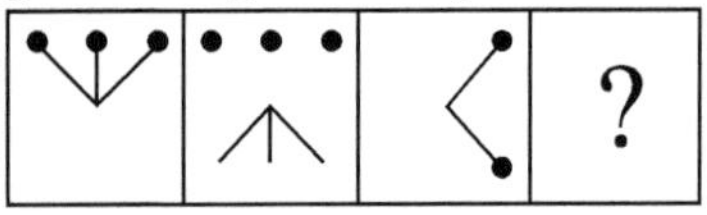

(A)  (B) 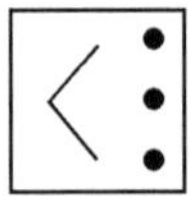

(C) 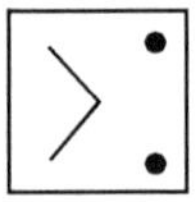 (D) 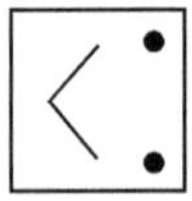

7. Identify the set of the series which follows the following rule.

Rule: The number of sectors of the circle increases as the size of circle decreases.

(A) 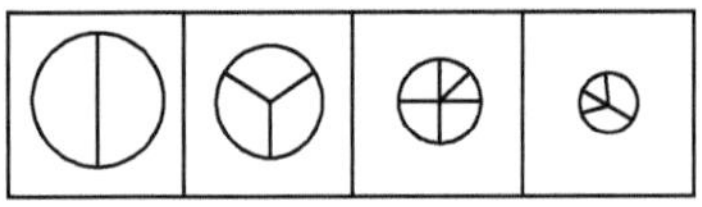

(B) 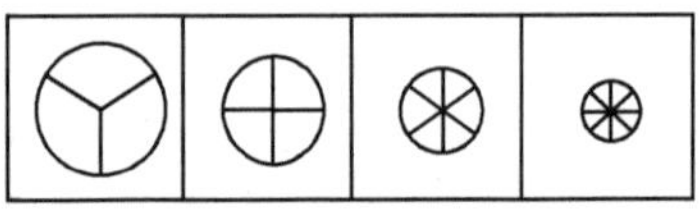

(C) 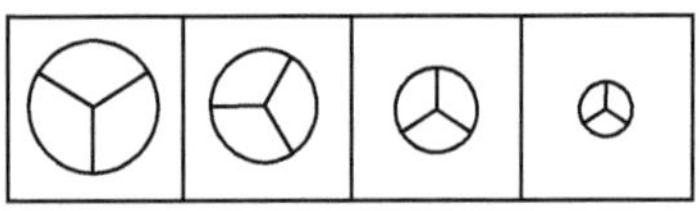

(D) 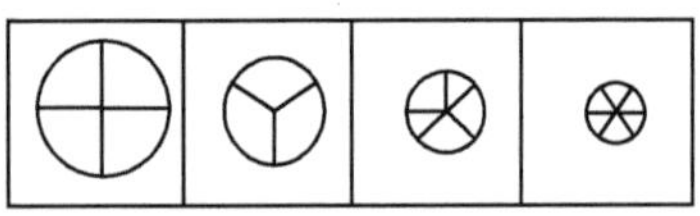

8. Identify the water image of the given figure.

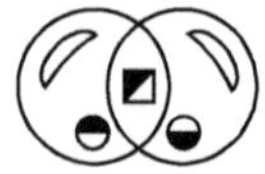

(A) 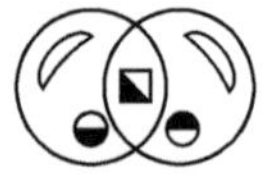 (B) 

(C) 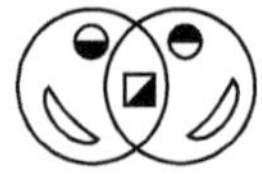 (D) 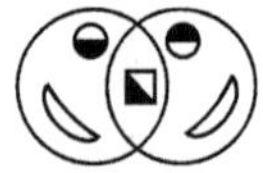

9. Can you count the number of squares present in the following figure?

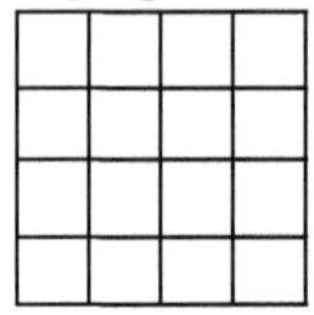

(A) 28 (B) 30
(C) 32 (D) 34

10. Identify the suitable figure to complete the following pattern.

(A)  (B) 

(C) 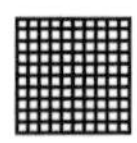 (D) 

SCIENCE

11. Identify the effect which does not satisfy the category of force?
(A) Magnetic
(B) Electric
(C) Chemical
(D) None of these

12. When an individual let's say a deep sea diver dives into the sea, his ears get hurt when he is deep inside the water. Why this pain is generated?
(A) Due to decrease in the atmospheric pressure
(B) Due to increase in the water pressure
(C) Due to limited supply of oxygen
(D) Due to salt of water.

13. When a meteor enters the Earth's atmosphere, it gets burnt. Why?
(A) Due to friction force of the air.
(B) Due to gravitational pull of the Earth.
(C) Due to excess heat energy of the Earth
(D) Due to transmitting solar radiations of the Earth.

14. Mark the disadvantage of the frictional force.
   (A) Wastage of heat energy
   (B) Production of noise through machines
   (C) Forest fires
   (D) All of these

15. What do you understand by sound travels in a medium. Mark the appropriate choice.
   (A) The medium travels along with the sound waves.
   (B) The source of the sound waves travels.
   (C) The medium travels with stationary sound waves.
   (D) The disturbance travels.

16. Arrange the following mediums in the descending order according to the speed of sound in that medium.
   (A) Gas > Liquid > Solid
   (B) Solid > Liquid > Gas
   (C) Liquid < Gas < Solid
   (D) Solid > gas > Liquid

17. Which of the following serves as the electrolyte in a dry cell?
   (A) Ammonium Chloride
   (B) Hydrochloric acid
   (C) Copper Sulphate
   (D) Zinc sulphate

18. The common voltage produced by the dry cell is ___________.
   (A) 15 V (B) 0.15 V
   (C) 1.5 V (D) 3 V

19. What happens in case of electric current flow through a conductor?
   (A) Some amount of kinetic energy is changed into the electrical energy.
   (B) Some amount of potential energy is converted into electrical energy
   (C) Some amount of kinetic energy is converted into heat energy
   (D) Some amount of electrical energy is converted into heat energy.

20. Which of the following is the correct S.I. unit of charge?
   (A) Ampere
   (B) Watt
   (C) Volt
   (D) Coulomb

21. Suppose a glass is rubbed against silk and an ebonite rod is rubbed with fur, then both rods are taken close to each other. What happens in such condition?
   (A) Both rods will repel each other
   (B) Both rods will attract each other
   (C) Ebonite rod will start behaving as magnet
   (D) Both rods will produce heat.

22. What is the arrangement of reflecting mirrors in a periscope?
   (A) Parallel to each other
   (B) At the right angle to each other
   (C) At the acute angle
   (D) Perpendicular to each other

23. What kind of image is formed at the retina of human eye?
   (A) Real and erect
   (B) Virtual and inverted
   (C) Real and inverted
   (D) Virtual and erect

24. Which of the following moons is the only moon with the active volcanoes?
   (A) Titan (B) Ganymede
   (C) Moon (D) Io

25. We are able to see some of the planets through our naked eyes, they are ___________.
   (A) Uranus, Neptune, Mars, Venus
   (B) Mars, Jupiter, Venus, Mercury
   (C) Venus, Neptune, Uranus, Mercury
   (D) We cannot see planets through our naked eyes.

26. The silk fibres are composed of ___________.
   (A) Protein (B) Body fat
   (C) Starch (D) Polysaccharides

27. Identify the property of thermosetting plastic.
(A) It is moldable
(B) It is fire resistant
(C) It is non- corrosive
(D) All of these

28. Two types of fibres are used to make which of the following fabrics?
(A) Nylon
(B) Polyester
(C) Polywool
(D) Rayon

29. How many electrons are generally found in the outermost shell of the non-metals?
(A) 8, 9, or 10
(B) 4, 5, 6 or 7
(C) 10, 20 or 30
(D) Cannot be determined

30. Identify the naturally occurring non-metal oxide.
(A) CO (B) NO_2
(C) SO_2 (D) All of these

31. Photographic films are made up of which compound?
(A) Silver chloride
(B) Silver bromide
(C) Copper bromide
(D) Copper iodide

32. Why kerosene oil is more suitable for burning oil lamps than the petrol?
(A) Kerosene consumes less amount of oxygen
(B) Kerosene is less polluting
(C) Kerosene is heavy than petrol
(D) Kerosene is less volatile

33. How is the gas of LPG cylinder liquified?
(A) By the application of high pressure
(B) By the application of low pressure
(C) By freezing the gas
(D) By the condensation of gas

34. LPG is a household gas which is used in the kitchen for cooking with the help of gas stove. If you have observed the flame of the gas you must have noticed a blue zone there. What is the meaning of this blue zone?
(A) Incomplete combustion zone
(B) Unburnt vapors zone
(C) Complete combustion zone
(D) Partial combustion zone

35. Identify the disadvantage(s) of the incomplete combustion of a fuel.
(A) Air pollution
(B) Production of harmful CO.
(C) Onset of breathing problems.
(D) All of these

36. Identify the correct %age amount of N, O and rare gases in the atmosphere.

	N	O	Rare gases
(A)	87	11	0.9
(B)	78	21	0.9
(C)	67	31	0.9

(D) It is not defined.

37. Some air pollutants such as CFC causes the depletion of ozone layer. What is the effect of CO?
(A) It also causes depletion of ozone layer
(B) It reduces the photosynthesis capacity of the plants
(C) It reduces the amount of oxygen in the blood
(D) All of these

38. Identify the example of integrated cultivation system.
(A) Production of phytoplankton invitro.
(B) Breeding of livestock on the oil palm plantation.
(C) Breeding of small fishes in the paddy fields
(D) All of these

39. Identify the modern technology in agriculture.
(A) Improvement of soil fertility by the use of synthetic chemicals.

(B) Production of high quality crops with the use of genetic engineering.
(C) Uses of agromachinery for various cultivation methods and procedures.
(D) All of these

40. Identify the largest organelle of a cell.
(A) Mitochondria
(B) Endoplasmic reticulum
(C) Nucleus
(D) Lysosomes

41. Which of the following intracellular transport structure helps in the synthesis of proteins and lipids?
(A) Endoplasmic reticulum
(B) Golgi complex
(C) Mitochondria
(D) Microtubules

42. What is the role of microorganisms in the field of biotechnology?
(A) In the field of gene therapy
(B) In the production of hormones
(C) In the brewery and food industry
(D) All of these

43. Occurrence of draught is followed by ____.
(A) Decreased food production
(B) Flooding
(C) Increased transpiration in plants
(D) Eutrophication

44. What is the correct sequence involved with the reproduction?
(A) Embryo → Foetus → Zygote → Baby
(B) Zygote → Embryo → Foetus → Baby
(C) Foetus → Zygote → Embryo → Baby
(D) Foetus→ Embryo →Zygote → Baby

45. Which of the blood enzymes is released by the pancreas?
(A) Insulin (B) Sucrase
(C) Cellulase (D) None of these

ACHIEVERS SECTION

46. Mark the correct sequence of the places as given in the following image, on the basis of increasing air pressure.

Sea Shore Mountains Triveni Sangam

(A) Mountains < Triveni Sangam < Sea Shore
(B) Mountains < Sea Shore < Triveni Sangam
(C) Triveni Sangam > Sea shore > Mountains
(D) Sea shore > Mountains > Triveni Sangam

47. Identify X and Y.

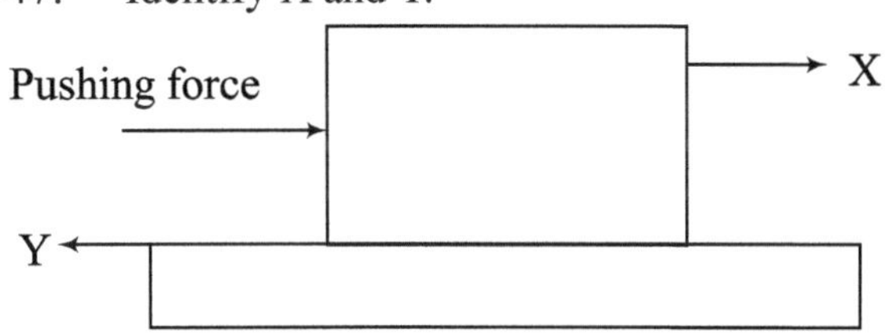

	X	Y
(A)	Displacement	Antifriction
(B)	Weight	Friction
(C)	Motion	Friction
(D)	Motion	Weight

48. Identify the correct statement on the basis of law of electrostatics.
   (A) A charged body is able to attract all kinds of charged or uncharged bodies.
   (B) A charged body always repels the body carrying opposite charge.
   (C) A charged body is always attracted by the similar charged body.
   (D) A charged body always attracts another charged body with opposite charge and repels the body carrying same charge.

49. What do you understand by a cosmic year?
   (A) The total time taken by Jupiter around the Sun.
   (B) The total taken by Io to revolve around Jupiter
   (C) The total time taken by the Sun to revolve around the center of milky way.
   (D) The time difference between two lunar eclipses occuring on the same date.

50. Match the column I with column II.

	Column I		Column II
1	Rope	a	Silk
2	Tiffin box	b	Acrylic
3	Sweater	c	Nylon
4	Saree	d	Plastic

	1	2	3	4
(A)	a	b	c	d
(B)	d	c	b	a
(C)	c	d	b	a
(D)	b	c	d	a

Mock Test Paper **2**

Total Questions : 50   Time : 1 Hour

N S O

NATIONAL SCIENCE OLYMPIAD

PATTERN AND MARKING SCHEME			
Section	**(1) Logical Reasoning**	**(2) Science**	**(3) Achievers Section**
No. of Questions	10	35	5
Marks per Questions	1	1	3

SYLLABUS

Section – 1: Verbal and Non-Verbal Reasoning.

Section – 2: Crop Production and Management, Microorganisms, Synthetic Fibres and Plastics, Metals and Non-metals, Coal and Petroleum, Combustion and Flame, Conservation of Plants and Animals,-Cell, Reproduction and Endocrine System,Force and Pressure, Friction, Sound, Chemical Effects of Electric Current, Some Natural Phenomena, Light, Stars and the Solar System, Pollution of Air and Water.

Section – 3: Higher Order Thinking Questions – Syllabus as per Section – 2.

LOGICAL REASONING

1. Identify the figure which is best suitable to continue the series.

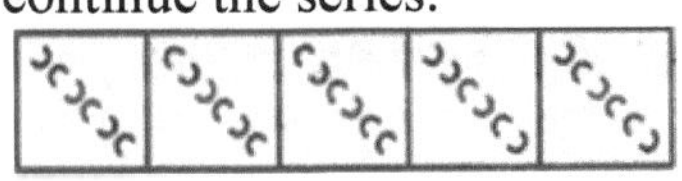

(A)  (B) 

(C) 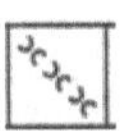 (D) 

2. Identify the odd one out.

(A)  (B) 

(C)  (D) 

3. Identify the mirror image of the given combination.

AN54WMG3

(A) 

(B) 

(C) 

(D) 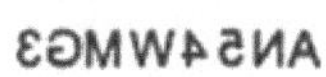

4. Find out which of the following images is possible with the given pieces.

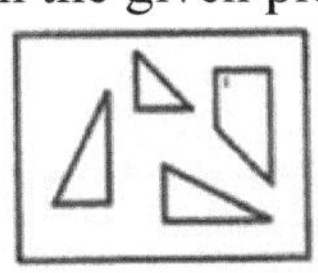

(A) 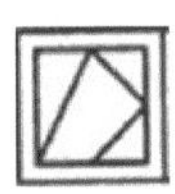 (B) 

(C)  (D) 

5. Identify the correct option which depicts the folded form of the given image. Dotted lines represent the point of paper folding.

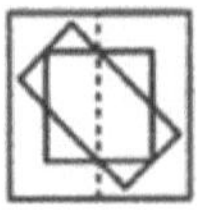

(A)  (B) 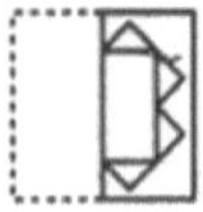

(C)  (D) 

6. Ratna left her home and started walking towards North and moved upto 15 km. She turned left and covered distance of 10 km. Then she turned to left and walked upto 5 km. At the end she turned towards East and walked upto 10 kms. Determine the direction of Ratna with respect to her house.
   (A) East (B) West
   (C) North (D) South

7. In a class there are seven students (including boys and girls) Ayan, Beenish, Chetna, Divya, Ekansh, Faiz and Ganga. They sit on three benches I, II and III such that at least two students on each bench and at least one girl on each bench. Chetna who is a girl student, does not sit with Ayan, Eesha and Divya. Faiz the boy student sits with only Beenish. Ayan sits on the bench I with his best friends. Ganga sits on the bench III. Ekansh is the brother of Chetna.

   On the basis of given information identify who sits with Chetna.
   (A) Ekansh (B) Beenish
   (C) Faiz (D) Ganga

8. Pointing towards Rohan, Aditi said, "He is the only son of the mother of my mother." Determine the relationship between Rohan and Aditi.
   (A) Rohan is maternal uncle of Aditi
   (B) Rohan is nephew of Aditi
   (C) Rohan and Aditi are siblings.
   (D) Cannot be determined.

9. Arun is 3 years elder than Babita and 3 years younger to Charles, while Babita and Damanjet are of same age. Calculate the age difference between Charles and Damanjeet.
   (A) 8 (B) 7
   (C) 3 (D) 6

10. What would come in the place of question mark?

A_2	C_4	E_6
G_3	I_5	?
M_5	O_9	Q_{14}

   (A) K8 (B) K15
   (C) L8 (D) L15

SCIENCE

11. Which endocrine gland is situated closest to the heart?
   (A) Pituitary
   (B) Thyroid
   (C) Hypothalamus
   (D) Thymus

12. What is the importance of the amniotic fluid present around the foetus?
   (A) It provides pre-birth immunity to the foetus
   (B) It provides immunity to the pregnant mother
   (C) It serves as the shock absorbent for the foetus
   (D) It provides nutrition to the foetus

13. What is the direction of flow of energy in an ecosystem?
   (A) Circular
   (B) Bidirectional
   (C) Unidirectional
   (D) No fixed direction.

14. Which of the following statements correctly defines bacteriophages?
   (A) It is plant pathogenic strain of bacteria.
   (B) It is a virus eating strain of bacteria.
   (C) It is bacteria killing strain of virus.
   (D) None of these

15. Identify the correct definition of the cell.
   (A) It is the initiating point of the life.
   (B) It is the structural and functional unit of life.
   (C) It is the smallest unit of the living beings.
   (D) All of these

16. The carbohydrate of the plasma membrane is involved in which function?
   (A) Identical cell repulsion
   (B) Passive transport
   (C) Cellular recognition
   (D) Active transport

17. Separation of chaff from grain is known as__________.
   (A) Winnowing (B) Harvesting
   (C) Threshing (D) Weeding

18. Determine the correct order of agricultural procedures and practices of the cultivation.
   (A) Ploughing, levelling, manuring, sowing, irrigation and harvesting
   (B) Sowing, irrigation, ploughing, levelling, manuring and harvesting
   (C) Irrigation, ploughing, levelling, manuring, sowing and harvesting
   (D) Ploughing, levelling, , irrigation, harvesting,manuring and sowing,

19. Identify the main source of sulphur dioxide emissions.
   (A) Petroleum refineries
   (B) Thermal power plants
   (C) Household activities
   (D) Water pollution

20. Lead particles are very common air and soil pollutants, how are these particles released into the air?
   (A) Burning of LPG
   (B) Burning of the organic matter
   (C) Burning of the petrol in automobiles.
   (D) None of these

21. Suppose, if total carbon dioxide of the atmosphere is removed then what will happen with the temperature of the Earth?
   (A) The temperature of the Earth will become very high
   (B) The temperature of the Earth will become very low.
   (C) There will be no effect on the temperature.
   (D) None of these

22. The heat produced after burning of a particular amount of the fuel is known as_________.
   (A) Condensing capacity
   (B) Vapor capacity
   (C) Heat density
   (D) Calorific value

23. A substance burns at a particular ignition temperature, if the temperature lowers down, then what will happen with the burning substance?
   (A) The flame of the substance will start flickering.
   (B) The substance will get extinguished.
   (C) The substance will start consuming more oxygen.
   (D) There will be no effect on the burning substance.

24. What temperature is applied on the crude petroleum during the process of fractional distillation?
(A) 400 – 500°C
(B) 200 – 300°C
(C) 100 – 200°C
(D) 900 – 1000°C

25. In the process of fractional distillation of petroleum, the vapours obtained at the highest boiling point get condensed at ____.
(A) Lowermost portion of the fractionating column
(B) Uppermost portion of the fractionating column
(C) In the middle portion of the fractionating column
(D) Cannot be determined

26. How many electrons are generally found in the outermost shell of the metals?
(A) 4, 5, 6, 7
(B) 1, 2, 3
(C) 8, 9, 10
(D) Depends on the type of metal

27. During the process of vulcanisation which of the following metals is used?
(A) Chlorine (B) Nitrogen
(C) Sulphur (D) All of these

28. Mark the correct option which is true regarding the order of metal reactivity.
(A) Al > Zn > Fe
(B) Al > Ca > Na
(C) Ag > Au > Na
(D) Pb > Al > Cu

29. Which of the following processes is used for the formation of polythene?
(A) Hydrogenation
(B) Isomerization
(C) Polymerization
(D) All of these

30. Identify the false statement.
(A) Thermoplastics behaves as the good conductor of electricity and heat.
(B) Thermoplastics are fire resistant.
(C) Thermoplastics are used to produce heat resistant substances.
(D) None of these

31. Which of the following materials is generally used to prepare some synthetic fibres such as acrylic or polyester?
(A) Petrochemicals
(B) Coconut fibers
(C) Synthetic fibers
(D) Plastic pulp

32. Which of the following planets was farthest from the Sun in the duration of 1979 to 1999?
(A) Uranus (B) Mars
(C) Earth (D) Neptune

33. Which of the following is behind the live telecast of your favourite sport on the TV?
(A) Polar satellites
(B) Natural satellites
(C) Geostationary satellite
(D) None of these

34. Identify the correct statement regarding lateral inversion?
(A) The left side of the object is on the right side of the image.
(B) The left side of the object is on the left side of the image.
(C) Both (A) and (B)
(D) None of these

35. Which of the following countries is most prone to the earthquakes?
(A) Nepal (B) Japan
(C) India (D) China

36. When a polyester or woollen cloth is rubbed against our body, it produces a crackling sound or even a spark. Which of the following factors is responsible for this phenomenon?
(A) Positive ions
(B) Friction

(C) Static electricity
(D) Earthing

37. Which of the following metals make an alloy named as Nichrome?
(A) Nitrogen and chromium
(B) Nitrogen, copper and manganese
(C) Nickle, copper and manganese
(D) Nickle and chromium

38. Which of the following is the correct definition of insulator?
(A) The materials which insulates our body during the winters.
(B) The materials which convert the electricity into the heat energy.
(C) The materials which conduct a huge amount of electricity in the same time.
(D) The materials which do not conduct the electricity.

39. Which of the following is a charge carrier in an electrolytic solution?
(A) Electrons (B) Protons
(C) Nucleus (D) Ions

40. Fill in the blanks.
Hertz is the unit of ___ and it can be alternatively represented as___.
(A) Sound, min-1 (B) Frequency, sec-1
(C) Sound, sec-1 (D) Frequency, m-1

41. Intensity or loudness of sound is dependent on which of the following factors?
(A) The vibrations of the sound waves.
(B) The distance between the destination and source of the sound waves.
(C) The amplitude of the sound waves.
(D) None of these

42. While walking on the ice we are advised to take one small step at a time to prevent ourselves from slipping. Why?
(A) Smaller step produces small friction.
(B) Small step helps us to secure our energy.
(C) Smaller steps ensure larger friction.
(D) Less body heat is burnt.

43. Mark the incorrect statement.
(A) If sliding motion is converted into rolling motion, friction is reduced.
(B) It is possible to reduce the friction force upto zero unit.
(C) Streamline shape of the organisms and other objects can reduce its friction with air and water.
(D) Friction force of a polished surface is minimum.

44. Which of the following is an example(s) of low pressure in everyday life?
(A) Carrying a school bag full of books and notebooks.
(B) Cutting your nails
(C) Air pressure in the wheel of cars.
(D) All of these

45. While playing the pin ball game you have to slide a ball in a lane to hit the pins. How does the force exerted on the bowling ball effect the pins?
(A) The position of the stationary pins changes.
(B) The shape of the stationary pins changes.
(C) The stationary pins remain unaffected.
(D) None of these

ACHIEVERS SECTION

46. For the description of a girl's scream into frequency and pitch, identify the correct set.
(A) High frequency, high pitch
(B) High frequency, low pitch
(C) Low frequency, high pitch
(D) Low frequency, low pitch

47. In the modern era of electricity evolution, the bulbs have been replaced by LEDs. Identify the correct option (s) regarding the reason.

a: LEDs have longer life than bulbs.

b: LEDs consumes less power than bulb

c: LEDs are less expensive than bulbs.

(A) a and c (B) b and c

(C) a and b (D) None of these

48. Calculate the angle between the reflected ray and incident ray.

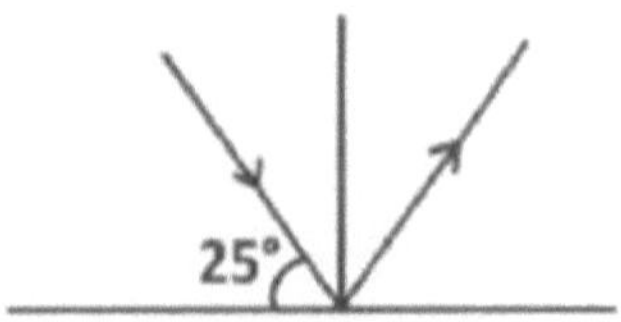

(A) 65° (B) 130°

(C) 45° (D) 90°

49. Identify the chemical displacement reaction.

(A) $2\ Na + Cl_2 \xrightarrow{Heat} 2NaCl$

(B) $2\ Al + Fe_2O_3 \xrightarrow{Heat} Al_2O_3 + 2\ Fe + Heat$

(C) Both (A) and (B)

(D) None of these

50. Identify the ill effect of green revolution.

(A) Improvement in the agriculture industry

(B) Dependency on the weedicides, pesticides, and fertilizers

(C) Both (A) and (B)

(D) None of these

NATIONAL CYBER OLYMPIAD (NCO)

Mock Test Paper 1

NCO

NATIONAL CYBER OLYMPIAD

Total Questions : 50 Time : 1 Hour

PATTERN AND MARKING SCHEME			
Section	**(1) Logical Reasoning**	**(2) Computer and IT**	**(3) Achievers Section**
No. of Questions	10	35	5
Marks per Questions	1	1	3

SYLLABUS

Section – 1: Verbal and Non-Verbal Reasoning

Section – 2: Fundamentals of Computers, Internet & Viruses, HTML-[Html, Head, Title, Body (Attributes: Background, Bgcolor, Text, Link, Alink, Vlink), Font, Center, BR, HR, Comment tag , Html Elements}, Flash CS6, MS Access, Networking, MS Word (Exploring File tab, Language and Translate options, Tracking features -Comments, Reviewing Pane, Tracking Changes, Comparing, Combining and Protecting documents, Working with References), MS PowerPoint (Exploring File tab and Slide Show tab, Comparing, Combining and Protecting presentations), MS Excel (Exploring File tab, Useful Formulas and Functions - IF, Even, Odd, LCM, GCD, Power, Product, Round, Sqrt, Sum, Min, Max, Average, Count, Upper, Lower And Replace, Cell referencing, Using Defined Names group), Memory & Storage Devices, Basics of Cyber Crimes, Cyber Laws, Operating Systems (Introduction, Features, Types-single user and multi-user), Latest Developments in the field of IT.

Section – 3: Higher Order Thinking Questions – Syllabus as per Section – 2.

LOGICAL REASONING

1. Choose one from the following that can replace the question mark.
   3, 4, 15, ?, 567
   (A) 64 (B) 80
   (C) 50 (D) 65

2. Amongst the following, choose one that represents similar relationship as 'PETAL' has with 'TELPA'.
   (A) BOWLS : WOSLB
   (B) JOKER : KOJRE
   (C) ENJOY : JNYEO
   (D) PROXY : ORXPY

3. In a certain language, if 'monitor' is coded 'keyboard', 'keyboard' is coded as 'desk' and 'desk' is coded as 'watch'. Then which of the following is useful to type?
   (A) Desk (B) Watch
   (C) Keyboard (D) Monitor

4. Pointing towards a child, Umang said, "She is the daughter of the only daughter of my mother". How is Umang related to that child?
   (A) Father (B) Brother
   (C) Grandfather (D) Uncle

5. Rohit starts walking from his house and walks 8 meters towards North. Then, he turns towards South and walks 4 meters. Then, he turns towards east and walks 3 meters. How far and in which direction is he with reference to his house?
(A) 17 meters East
(B) 9 meters North-East
(C) 5 meters North-East
(D) 9 meters South-East

6. Choose one from the following that gives the minimum number of straight lines required to make the given figure.

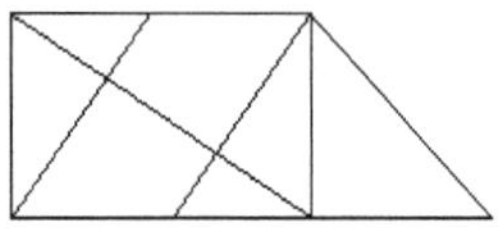

(A) 9 (B) 8
(C) 11 (D) 10

7. Choose one of the following that indicates the best relation between Wood, Chair and Cup.

(A) 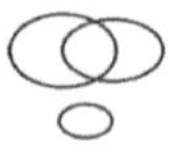 (B) 

(C)  (D) 

8. If and , then what will be the correct value of ?
(A) 8 (B) 6
(C) 4 (D) 2

9. The given diagram shows a transparent circular sheet with a design and a dotted line on it. The sheet is required to be folded along the dotted line. Choose one of the following figure that is similar to folded form of the given sheet.

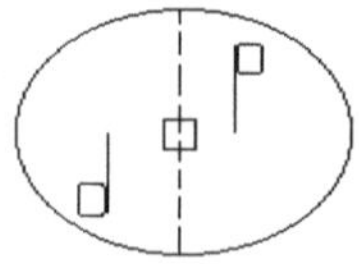

(A) 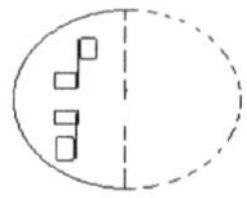 (B) 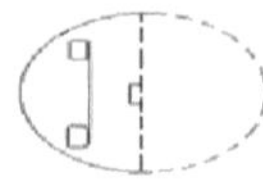

(C) 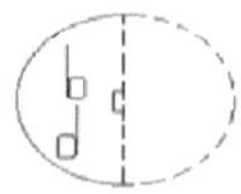 (D) 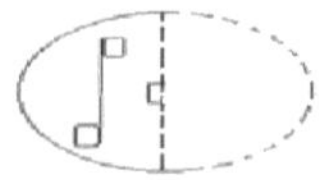

10. Which one of the following figures from the options satisfies the same conditions of placement of dots as in the figure given in the question?

(A) 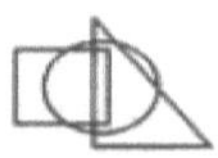 (B) 

(C) 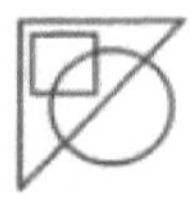 (D) 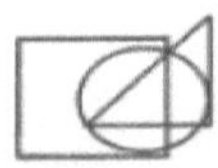

COMPUTERS AND IT

11. Which one of the following is a spreadsheet application?
(A) MS Word (B) MS Paint
(C) MS Excel (D) MS Access

12. Choose the type of memory that is used to stored BIOS instructions, embedded in the computer motherboard.
(A) ROM (B) SRAM
(C) RAM (D) DRAM

13. Which of the following tag defines the title of the work?
(A) <code> (B) <address>
(C) <dfn> (D) <cite>

14. Select one from the following that is used to create an unordered list.
(A) <dl> (B) <ol>
(C) <li> (D) <ul>

15. Which one of the following tools is used to select an object in free form?

(A)  (B) 

(C)  (D) 

16. Which of the following feature of MS word is used to find the similar meaning of a word?

(A)  (B) 

(C)  (D) 

17. Alt+Ctrl+M is used to m __________.
(A) Increase the file size.
(B) Reduce the file size.
(C) Insert a new comment in a document.
(D) Delete a comment from the document.

18. Which of the following is the function of the given feature of MS PowerPoint?

(A) Hide a slide from the presentation.
(B) Adjust spacing between characters.
(C) Change the font size.
(D) change the font style

19. Select one of the following features of MS PowerPoint that is used to hide a slide from the presentation.

(A)  (B) 

(C)  (D) 

20. Choose the incorrect statement about the slide show view in MS PowerPoint.
(A) Insert Key cannot be used to go to the next slide in slide show view.
(B) Insert Key can be used to go to the previous slide in slide show view.
(C) Enter key can be used to go to the next slide in slide show view.
(D) Backspace key can be used to go to the previous slide in slide show view.

21. Which one of the following peripherals allows users to connect a device to a computer?
(A) Plug and Play (B) Off and On
(C) Click and Ejec (D) Push and Pop

22. Which one of the following is not a software?
(A) MS Office
(B) Firmware
(C) Firefox
(D) Central processing Unit

23. Choose the Volatile type of memory from the following.
(A) Hard disc (B) Magnetic tape
(C) SRAM (D) Floppy disc

24. In which memory of the computer, the data in current use is stored?
(A) PROM (B) RAM
(C) DPROM (D) EEPROM

25. Which attribute of <img> tag adds space to the left and right side of an image?
(A) hspace (B) ismap
(C) srcset (D) lowsrc

26. Choose the option that gives the correct name for the tool given below.

(A) Selection tool
(B) Sub-selection tool
(C) Lasso tool
(D) Free transform tool

27. Keystroke 'Alt + F4' is used to __________.
(A) Open start menu
(B) Close an active window
(C) Open a new tab
(D) Switch between tabs

28. What is the function of the given feature of MS word?

(A) Check the document for any password protection method.
(B) Increase the file size.
(C) Convert the selected text into a hyper-link.
(D) Recover unsaved documents.

29. The sum of cells A1 through A59 is the output of ________________.
(A) =SUM(A1:A59)
(B) =SUM(A1:A60)
(C) =SUM(A1:A58)
(D) =SUM(A2:A59)

30. Which one of the following functions displays the sum of selected cells in MS Excel?
(A) 
(B) 
(C) 
(D) 

31. = TODAY() in MS Excel is used to ______.
(A) enter current date and time
(B) enter current date
(C) enter current day
(D) enter the current month

32. By which name, the rows in MS Access are known?
(A) Fields (B) Objects
(C) Records (D) Lines

33. In MS Access, Home tab→Sort & Filter Group→Filter is used to access ________.
(A) Filter (B) Design view
(C) Sort (D) Selection

34. What is the function of the given feature of MS Access?

(A) Launch the option Tab box
(B) Launch the label wizard
(C) Launch the Query wizard
(D) Launch the report wizard

35. Which of the following web page is delivered directly to the user exactly as stored?
(A) Server-side dynamic web page
(B) Static web page
(C) Client-side dynamic web page
(D) None of these

36. Choose one from the following which is not a search engine.
(A) Google (B) DuckDuckGo
(C) Yahoo (D) Opera Mini

37. Which one of the following is not used to communicate online with friends?
(A) Facebook (B) WhatsApp
(C) Amazon (D) Skype

38. Choose one from the following that is used to represent Tree topology.
(A) 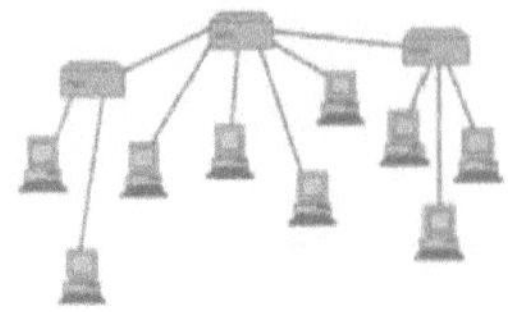
(B) 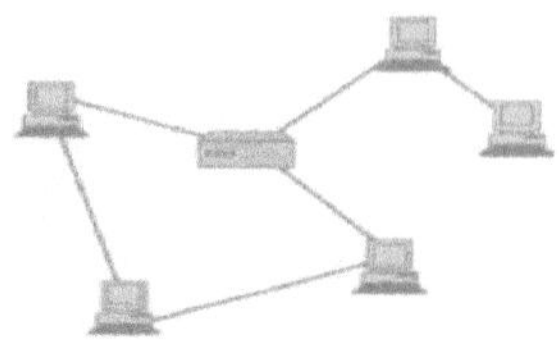
(C) 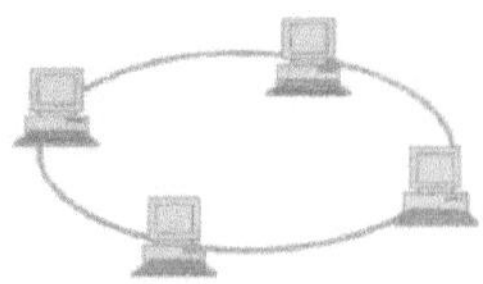
(D) None of these

39. By which another name, an Ethernet network is known?
(A) Connecting network
(B) Wired network
(C) Extension network
(D) All of the above

40. What does OSI stand for?
(A) Overall system Interconnection
(B) Open system Internet
(C) Open System Interconnection
(D) Open server Interconnection

41. Which one of the following allows user to send and receive money from mobile devices?
(A) Flipkart (B) Hike
(C) Line (D) Google wallet

42. For what use, the proximity sensor is used in mobile phones?
    (A) To detect the presence of nearby objects without any physical contact.
    (B) To provide location and time information.
    (C) To provide levels of enhanced security.
    (D) To detect the orientation of the phone

43. Choose an operating system that allows a user to perform more than one task at the same time.
    (A) Multi-user operating system
    (B) Multi-tasking operating system
    (C) Multi-server operating system
    (D) Single-user operating system

44. Select one from the following that is not a threat for electronic payment system.
    (A) Trojan horse
    (B) Computer worms
    (C) Computer virus
    (D) Firewall

45. Which of the following is used to protect unauthorized access to your computer?
    (A) Spyware (B) Malware
    (C) Firewall (D) Trojan horse

ACHIEVERS SECTION

46. Which technique is used for input text into a computer by means of a document reader?
    (A) OMR
    (B) OCR
    (C) Smart Card
    (D) Voice recognition

47. Select the correct statement regarding the hard disc.
    (A) Hard disc is a volatile and sequential access memory device.
    (B) Hard disc is a volatile and non-sequential access memory device.
    (C) Hard disc is a non-volatile and non-sequential access memory device.
    (D) Hard disc is a non-volatile and sequential access memory device.

48. Identify the feature of MS Word.

    It combines revisions from multiple authors into a single document.

    It compares two different versions of a document.
    (A) Track changes
    (B) Compare
    (C) Recent pane
    (D) Display for review

49. Select the use of the given feature of MS PowerPoint.

    (A) It automatically updates slides in the handout when the presentation changes.
    (B) Record the total number of slides in the presentation.
    (C) Check the presentation for content that people with disabilities might find difficult to read.
    (D) Save the presentation in a fixed format.

50. Match the functions of MS Excel given in column-I with their uses given in column-II.

Column I		Column II	
a.	COUNTA	(i)	Count all values in a range
b.	ROUNDUP	(ii)	Adds up all the values in a range
c.	SUM	(iii)	Count all non-empty cells in a range
d.	COUNT	(iv)	Round a number up to a specified number of digits

(A) a-(i), b-(iv), c-(ii), d-(iii)
(B) a-(i), b-(ii), c-(iv), d-(iii)
(C) a-(iii), b-(iv), c-(i), d-(ii)
(D) a-(iii), b-(iv), c-(ii), d-(i)

Mock Test Paper 2

NCO

NATIONAL CYBER OLYMPIAD

Total Questions : 50 Time : 1 Hour

PATTERN AND MARKING SCHEME			
Section	**(1) Logical Reasoning**	**(2) Computer and IT**	**(3) Achievers Section**
No. of Questions	10	35	5
Marks per Questions	1	1	3

SYLLABUS

Section – 1: Verbal and Non-Verbal Reasoning

Section – 2: Fundamentals of Computers, Internet & Viruses, HTML-[Html, Head, Title, Body (Attributes: Background, Bgcolor, Text, Link, Alink, Vlink), Font, Center, BR, HR, Comment tag , Html Elements}, Flash CS6, MS Access, Networking, MS Word (Exploring File tab, Language and Translate options, Tracking features -Comments, Reviewing Pane, Tracking Changes, Comparing, Combining and Protecting documents, Working with References), MS PowerPoint (Exploring File tab and Slide Show tab, Comparing, Combining and Protecting presentations), MS Excel (Exploring File tab, Useful Formulas and Functions - IF, Even, Odd, LCM, GCD, Power, Product, Round, Sqrt, Sum, Min, Max, Average, Count, Upper, Lower And Replace, Cell referencing, Using Defined Names group), Memory & Storage Devices, Basics of Cyber Crimes, Cyber Laws, Operating Systems (Introduction, Features, Types-single user and multi-user), Latest Developments in the field of IT.

Section – 3: Higher Order Thinking Questions – Syllabus as per Section – 2.

LOGICAL REASONING

1. Which one of the following can complete the given series?

   3, 7, 13, 11, 15, 13, 19, ?

   (A) 23 (B) 13
   (C) 17 (D) 21

2. Choose one of the following that can replace the question mark.

   CG : IM :: FJ : ?

   (A) LO (B) LR
   (C) LN (D) LP

3. In a certain coding system, 'AREA' is coded as 'EWKH' and 'ROOF' is coded as 'VTUM'. How is 'HOME' written in the same code?

   (A) LTSM (B) LSTL
   (C) LTSL (D) LTRL

4. If A@B means A is the father of B, A#B means A is the brother of B, A%B means A is the mother of B and A$B means A is the sister of B. Then which of the following relation is indicated by P#Q%R$S?

   (A) P is father of S
   (B) P is maternal uncle of S
   (C) Q is father of R
   (D) P is maternal aunt of S

5. If Raman is 5 meters to the South-West of Rohit, Rahul is 6 meters to the East of Raman and also 7 meters to the South-East of Rohit. If Raj is 10 meters to the North of Rahul, then in which direction of Rohit is Raj standing?

   (A) South-East (B) North
   (C) North-East (D) South-West

6. Which one of the following gives the correct number of triangles in the given figure?

(A) 28 (B) 22
(C) 20 (D) 26

7. In a row of boys, Rahul is sitting at 14th position from the left end of the row. If he will be shifted towards the right end of the row by 5 places, he will be at 7th position from the right end of the row. How many boys are there in the row?

(A) 26 (B) 25
(C) 24 (D) 27

8. Which one of the following images is the water image of the given combination of letters and numbers

(A) 

(B) 

(C) 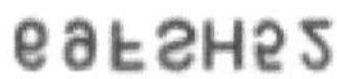

(D) 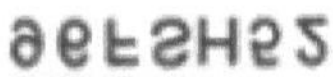

9. Choose an alternative figure that contains figure (A) as its part.

(X)

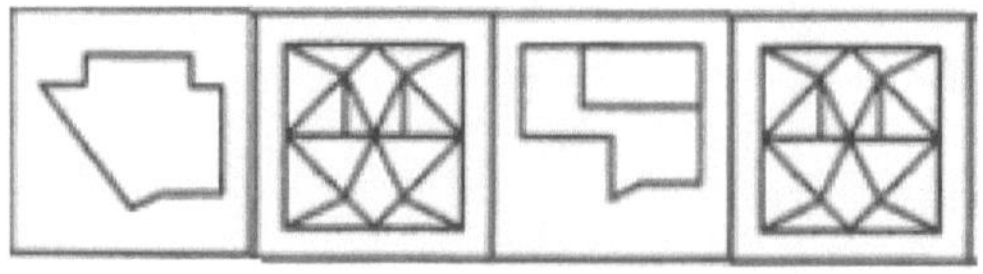

(1) (2) (3) (4)

(A) (2) (B) (1)
(C) (4) (D) (3)

10. Two different positions of dice are shown in the figure given below. Observe the dots on the dice and find the total number of dots on the face opposite to the face containing four dots.

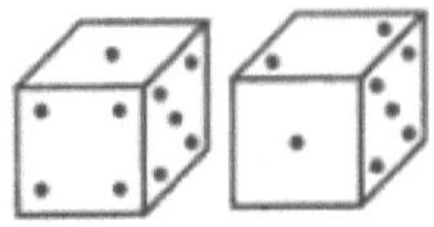

(A) 2 (B) 3
(C) 6 (D) 4

COMPUTERS AND IT

11. Which programming language can be understood by the computers without any translator?
(A) Assembly language
(B) Machine language
(C) High level language
(D) Fourth generation language

12. How many kilobytes are there in 54 MB?
(A) 55,296 kilobytes
(B) 5400 kilobytes
(C) 54000 kilobytes
(D) 27000 kilobytes

13. Which of the following tag is used to put a horizontal line in HTML?
(A) <hr> (B) <Line>
(C) <P> (D)

14. Bgcolor is an attribute of <body> tag that is used to specify the ________________ of the document.
(A) Text
(B) Size
(C) Background
(D) Background colour

15. Which one of the following is the function of the keystroke, Ctrl + F8?
(A) Open a new window
(B) Create a new symbol
(C) Switch between tabs
(D) Close active documents

16. Select one that can be accessed by going to Review tab→ Tracking group.

(A)  (B) 

(C)  (D) 

17. Which of the following is the function of 'Insert tab→Links group→Bookmark'?
(A) Display of Review
(B) Open Bookmark window
(C) Comparing documents
(D) Close Bookmark window

18. Which one of the following is a use of 'Presenter view' in MS PowerPoint?
(A) Display a presentation on two monitors
(B) Hide an unwanted slide from the presentation.
(C) Open 'Header and Footer' window from Backstage view.
(D) Broadcast a presentation on the internet.

19. Select one from the following that can be used to show play controls during the slide show.
(A) Slide Show tab→Set Up→Group→-Show Media Controls
(B) Slide Show tab→Settings→Group→-Show Media Controls
(C) Slide Show tab→display→Group→-Show Media Controls
(D) Slide Show tab→Start Slide Show→Group→Show Media Controls

20. What is the function of the given save & send feature of the MS PowerPoint?

(A) View a slide without PowerPoint.
(B) Change the show type of the presentation from 'Presented by a speaker' to 'Browsed at a Kiosk'.
(C) Create a full-fidelity video from the current presentation.
(D) Recover unsaved presentation.

21. Which one of the following software is used by products like remote control, digital watches and microwave ovens?
(A) Net software (B) Firmware
(C) Middleware (D) None of these

22. Which output device is used for the presentation or for viewing videos?
(A) Printer (B) Film recorder
(C) Plotter (D) Projector

23. What is the full form of NVRAM?
(A) Non-valuable random-access memory
(B) Non-viewable random-access memory
(C) Non-volatile random-access memory
(D) Non-volatile read access memory

24. Choose the memory from the following that is used in portable devices such as tablets and mobile phones?
(A) SD card (B) Hard disc
(C) CD (D) DVD

25. <li> and </li> in HTML is used to ______.
(A) display the items in bold form
(B) make the text in italic form
(C) make the text Inline
(D) display the items in bulleted form.

26. Select one of the following that allows a user to view several frames when creating animations in Adobe Flash CS6.
(A) Layer (B) Onion skin
(C) Locking (D) Masking

27. Which of the following is the function of hand tool?
(A) Give color to the outline of an object
(B) Zoom in and Zoom out the view of the movie.
(C) Move the stage in all direction without changing the magnification.
(D) Select an object in free form.

28. In MS word, Ctrl + Shift + P is used to ____________.
(A) Change the font size
(B) Apply the Normal style
(C) Change the font
(D) Reduce a hanging indent

29. Which of the following is NOT a cause of NULL error in MS Excel?
(A) The specified ranges do not intersect.
(B) The start and the end points of cell ranges are separated by a space
(C) Individual cell references in a formula are separated by a space.
(D) The formula is trying to multiply a value.

30. What is the function of given feature of MS Excel?

(A) Create, edit and delete names used in the workbook.
(B) Display the sum of selected cells.
(C) Search a value in a table.
(D) Change the format of a cell.

31. Select an Invalid function of MS excel from the following options.
(A) COUNTIFS (B) COUNTUP
(C) COUNTIF (D) COUNTA

32. Which of the following is the function of Queries in MS Access?
(A) To write and fill up the data.
(B) To view, change and analyse data in different ways.
(C) To enter the information for one record at a time.
(D) None of these

33. Which one of the following can be accessed by 'External Tab→Collect data→Manage Replies' in MS Access?
(A) Query Wizard (B) Design view
(C) Field box (D) Manage replies

34. Select one from the following that represents Design View in MS Access.
(A)  (B) 
(C)  (D) 

35. Select one from the following that is the correct full form of HTML?
(A) Hypertext Makeup Language
(B) Hypertext Machine Language
(C) Hypertext Markup Language
(D) Hypertext Modern Language

36. By which another name, Web 3.0 is known?
(A) The static web (B) The semantic web
(C) The interweb (D) None of these

37. Which one of the following should be deleted from the PC to erase cookies?
(A) Drivers Folder
(B) Web activity folder
(C) Temporary Internet files
(D) All of these

38. Among the following, which device forwards data packets between computer networks?
(A) Firewall (B) Pen drive
(C) Bridge (D) Router

39. What is the full form of FMTP?
(A) File Multicast Transport Protocol
(B) File Multicast Transform Protocol
(C) File Multiuser Transport Protocol
(D) File Multicast Terminate Protocol

40. In which network topology, each node is connected to exactly two other nodes to form a single continuous pathway for signals through each node?
(A) Star network topology
(B) Bus network topology
(C) Mesh network topology
(D) Ring network topology

41. Which of the following is represented by the given symbol?

(A) Facebook (B) Twitter
(C) Snapchat (D) Skype

42. What is the use of Smart Covers in tablet computers?
   (A) Connect tablet computer to PC.
   (B) Provide internet connectivity
   (C) Protect the touchscreen and save energy
   (D) Type and input a text through voice.

43. Find the odd one out.
   (A) Google
   (B) Apple MacOS
   (C) Microsoft Windows
   (D) Apple iOS

44. What is a key logger?
   (A) Antivirus (B) Firmware
   (C) Spyware (D) None of these

45. By which name, the first virus of the computer is known?
   (A) MacAfee (B) Creeper
   (C) Blaster (D) Sasser

ACHIEVERS SECTION

46. Which of the following statement is TRUE about the device given in the image?

   (A) The device shown in the image is known as Printer.
   (B) The device shown in the image is an output device.
   (C) The device shown in image accepts text and graphic output from a computer and transfer the information to the paper.
   (D) The device shown in the image is projector and it is an input device.

47. Identify the memory whose description is given below.

   A temporary memory that keeps certain data available for quick reference.

   It is a small sized type of computer volatile memory.
   (A) Cache memory (B) ROM
   (C) Hard disc (D) Magnetic tape

48. Which feature of MS word helps you to recover unsaved documents?
   (A) Track changes (B) Summary Pane
   (C) Recent Pane (D) Reviewing Pane

49. Match the icons of MS PowerPoint given in column-I with their functions given in column-II.

Column I		Column II	
a.		(i)	Record slide and animation timings.
b.		(ii)	Encrypt your document with password
c.		(iii)	Recover unsaved presentation.
d.		(iv)	Set up advanced options for the slide show.

   (A) a-(iii), b-(i), c-(ii), d-(iv)
   (B) a-(iv), b-(i), c-(ii), d-(iii)
   (C) a-(iv), b-(i), c-(iii), d-(ii)
   (D) a-(iv), b-(ii), c-(i), d-(iii)

50. Select the formula that should be used in the cell B2 to get 18% marks of the total marks.

	A	B
1	Total marks	Marks (18%)
2	800	

   (A) =A2*0.018 (B) =A2+(A2*0.18)
   (C) =A2*0.18 (D) =A2*(A2+0.18)

INTERNATIONAL ENGLISH OLYMPIAD (IEO)

Mock Test Paper 1

I E O

INTERNATIONAL ENGLISH OLYMPIAD

Total Questions : 50 Time : 1 Hour

PATTERN AND MARKING SCHEME				
Section	**(1) Word and Structure Knowledge**	**(2) Reading**	**(3) Spoken and Written Expression**	**(4)Achievers**
No. of Questions		45		5
Marks per Questions		1		3

SYLLABUS

Section – 1 : Synonyms, Antonyms, Analogies and Spellings, Collocations, Phrasal Verbs, Idioms or Proverbs, Homonyms and Homophones, One-Word, Nouns, Pronouns, Verbs, Adverbs, Adjectives, Articles, Prepositions, Prepositional Phrases, Participle Phrases, Conjunctions, Determiners, Jumbled Words and Punctuations, Tenses, Voices and Narrations, Question Tags, etc. Words related to Leisure, Household Items/Issues, Social Causes, Outdoor Locations and Activities, etc.

Section – 2 : Search for and retrieve information from various text types like News Reports, Blurb, Dictionaries, etc., Understand information presented in Instruction Manual Format, Message Format and others. Acquire broad understanding of and look for specific information in longer texts like Editorials, Essays, etc.

Section – 3 : Ability to understand situation-based variations in functions like Requesting, Giving Information, Expressing Surprise, Pronunciation etc.

Section – 4 : Higher Order Thinking Questions - Syllabus as per Sections 1, 2 and 3.

WORD AND STRUCTURE KNOWLEDGE

1. Insert the suitable question tag.

   Nitibha will come tonight, _____

   (A) willn't she? (B) won't she?
   (C) isn't it? (D) doesn't she?

2. Identify the correctly punctuated sentence.

   (A) I don't care about the exams.
   (B) I does not care about the exams!
   (C) I do not care about the exams!
   (D) I; don't care; about the exams.

3. Complete the sentence with the suitable participle.

   My daughter _____ to me many times.

   (A) has lied (B) have lied
   (C) will lied (D) have been

4. Complete the sentence with the prepositional phrase.

   Yuvraj Singh didn't let cancer discourage him _______ he began to fight against it.

   (A) On the other hand
   (B) On the contrary
   (C) On the opposition
   (D) Within the contrary

5. Change the speech of the following sentence.

   My niece said to me, "Good bye, aunty."

   (A) Aunty good bye, my niece told me.
   (B) My niece told me good bye aunty.
   (C) Good bye aunty, it was said by my niece.
   (D) My niece bid good bye to me.

6. Change the voice of the following sentence.

Don't make a noise in the class.

(A) Didn't make a noise in the class.

(B) The class should not make a noise.

(C) You are forbidden to make a noise in the class.

(D) It is not allowed to make a noise in the class.

7. Complete the tense with the correct choice.

Protein deficiency ______ Kwashiorkor

(A) causes into (B) results into

(C) develops into (D) arise into

8. Arrange the following jumbled words into a meaningful sentence.

zero / Indian/ invented/ famous/ is a/ who/ astronomer/ Aryabhata

(A) Aryabhata is a famous Indian astronomer who invented zero.

(B) Zero invented by Indian astronomer who is famous Aryabhata

(C) who is Aryabhata Indian invented famous zero.

(D) none of these

9. Insert the determiners to complete the sentence.

In ___ library all ___ books are placed on ___ fixed position.

(A) a, the, its

(B) the, of the, its

(C) a, the, his

(D) the, no determiner, their

10. Fill in the blank with suitable conjunctions.

____Vikrant ____ his friend had written this story.

(A) With, and

(B) Either, or

(C) A boy, and

(D) none of these

11. Insert the suitable preposition.

The class teacher said to the class, "Open your book ___ page no. 32."

(A) upon (B) within

(C) on (D) at

12. Insert the suitable articles in the blanks.

Doctors says that morning walk is ____ exercise for ___ healthy person, cure for sick and ____ tonic for ____ weak.

(A) an, the, a, the

(B) no article, the, a, the

(C) the, the, a, the

(D) an, the, no article, no article

13. Choose the most appropriate word which makes best combination with the adjective 'fixed'.

(A) price (B) time

(C) place (D) all of these

14. Take the help of the bracketed word to convert it into the most suitable adverb.

Though Kartik was not invited for the party but he showed up _______ (unexpected)

(A) exceptionally

(B) subexponentially

(C) unexpectedly

(D) none of these

15. Which of the following word represents the category of homonym?

(A) ideal (B) second

(C) special (D) either

16. Identify the set of true homophones.

(A) cymbal and symbol

(B) collie and collies

(C) care and air

(D) none of these

17. In India, which of the following place is centre of attraction for the foreigners?

(A) Amer Fort (B) Pink City

(C) Red Fort (D) Taj Mahal

18. Which of the following is the major household issue for the working mothers nowadays?

(A) Arguments with the boss.

(B) Stress due to overwork.

(C) Balance between work and homelife.
(D) None of these

19. Identify the set of adventurous outdoor activity.
(A) hiking, bungee jumping
(B) Scooba diving, river rafting
(C) camping, skiing
(D) all of these

20. What is the meaning of the phrasal verb 'bringing up'?
(A) to raise someone upto adulthood
(B) to admire someone
(C) to bring a gift for someone
(D) getting better day by day

21. Complete the sentence with suitable auxiliary verb.

You _____ produce sound while chewing something.

(A) Must	(B) Should
(C) Would	(D) Had

22. Fill in the blank with suitable interrogative pronoun.

_____ are you going in the coming summer break?

(A) When	(B) Where
(C) What	(D) Which

23. Replace the underlined word with the suitable common noun.

My brother is preparing hard to get admission in a top <u>place to study.</u>

(A) Cafeteria	(B) University
(C) Factory	(D) Organization

24. Which proverb is suitable for the following situation.

My mother told me to get some important household item from the groceries and my father told me to drop his parcel on the propriety. I took the parcel and after leaving the parcel I purchased groceries and came back home.

(A) Method to my madness.
(B) Far cry from.
(C) Al good things must come to an end.
(D) I killed two birds with one stone.

25. What is the meaning of the idiom 'raining cats and dogs'?
(A) It's raining heavily.
(B) The cat and dogs are running like the rain.
(C) Rain sounds like meow and thunder sounds like bark.
(D) It was raining for animals only.

26. Provide one word.

Something done or spoken without any preparation.

(A) Epilogue	(B) Dialogue
(C) Extempore	(D) Contemporary

27. Find the odd two out.

Hard, difficult, tough, soothing, painful, unsuitable, convenient, inconvenient unfavourable.

(A) hard and unsuitable
(B) soothing and convenient
(C) inconvenient and convenient
(D) tough and soothing

28. Find out the correct spelling.

(A) Flouresent	(B) Floroscent
(C) Floorsent	(D) Fluorescent

29. Antonym of melodious is:

(A) tough	(B) sweet
(C) harsh	(D) music

30. Which of the following is/are the synonym(s) of 'satisfaction'.

(A) Gratification	(B) Contentment
(C) Relish	(D) all of the above

Following is the blurb of the famous book 'Wings of the Fire.' Read it thoroughly and answer the questions.

"Wings of Fire" is the autobiography of Late APJ Abdul Kalam, who was an eminent scientist and former president of India. He was the most loved and most popular president of India. Arun Tiwari is the co- writer of the book. He was a man with the polite beginning, and he led a very simple life. he carried an unusual mix of spiritual convictions with man spirit of scientific enquiry. He was born in 1931 in Rameswaram (Tamil Nadu). He was born in to a Muslim family but had 'Sarvdharm Sambhav' for the all the religions. A young boy from a very small village, who started his journey as a newspaper hawker, hurled his fortune and became the "Missile Man' of India. Dr. Kalam took the reins at Defence Research and Development Organization (DRDO) and the Indian Space Research Organization (ISRO) and inspired generations through some of the most innovative, and breath taking scientific feats of independent India. His mastery in advanced science and space innovation has impelled India to end up a sparkling case for youthful countries needing to stamp their insight and aptitudes over the globe as well as the incomprehensibility of our Universe. In the starting of the book he paid his homage to his parents and especially his mother kalam named 'My mother'.

The book opens into four distinct parts named as-

1931 to 63- Orientation, 1963 to 80- Creation, 1981 to 91- Propitiation, Beyond 1991- Contemplation

31. Late APJ Abdul Kalam is fondly known as:
    (A) Missile man of India
    (B) Nuclear man of India
    (C) Space man of India
    (D) Iron man of India

32. Who is the co- writer of the book?
    (A) Arun Tiwari
    (B) Arun Mishra
    (C) Atul Tiwari
    (D) Atul Mishra

33. What is the full form of ISRO?
    (A) Indian Special Research Organization
    (B) Indian Space Research Organization
    (C) Indian Special Relevant Organization
    (D) India Special at Research Organization

34. What was Late APJ Kalam was master at?
    (A) Adherent Science and Space innovation
    (B) Advance science and astronaut research
    (C) Advance science and space innovation
    (D) None of these

Following are the headlines of a famous newspaper, when statue of unity was inaugurated. Read it carefully and answer the questions that follow.

Prime Minister Narendra Modi, dedicated to the nation a 182-metre statue of Sardar Vallabhbhai Patel, believed to be the tallest in the world and said it will be a reminder about the courage of a man who thwarted efforts to disintegrate India. In his speech, Modi stressed that the statue would generate immense employment opportunities for the local tribal living near the dam in Narmada district. Gujarat's governor OP Kohli, chief minister Vijay Rupani and BJP chief Amit Shah were also present at the unveiling of the Statue of Unity. PM Modi described the Statue of Unity as a symbol of the country's engineering and technical capabilities. To welcome visitors, the Gujarat government has not only built a 3-star hotel, shopping centre and a research centre in the Sardar Patel statue complex but has also built high-speed elevators that will take you to a height of about 400 feet through the core of the statue where you can get a panoramic view of the surroundings.

The imposing monument is twice the height of the Statue of Liberty in the US and is built on an islet, Sadhu Bet, around 3.5 km downstream from the Sardar Sarovar Dam in Gujarat's Narmada district. The best way to reach Sadhu Bet island is to take a boat ride. built at a cost of Rs. 2,989 crore, the statue depicts Sardar Vallabhbhai Patel, India's first home minister, wearing a traditional dhoti and shawl, towering over the Narmada River.

Padma Bhushan awardee, Ram Vanji Sutar, a 93-year-old acclaimed sculptor who graduated from the prestigious J.J School of Art in Bombay, designed the statue. He has sculpted masterpieces including that of Mother Chambal at Gandhi Sagar Dam in Madhya Pradesh, equestrian statue of Maharaja Ranjit Singh in Amritsar, and numerous statues of Mahatma Gandhi.

It has been built by Larsen and Toubro and the state-run Sardar Sarovar Narmada Nigam Ltd. It took about 250 engineers and 3,400 labourers to construct the statue. Malaysia-based Eversendai, which constructed Dubai's famous Burj Al Arab and Burj Khalifa buildings, was handed the contract for the steel framework. It has been built using over 70,000 tonnes of cement, 18,500 tonnes of reinforcement steel, 6,000 tonnes of structural steel and 1,700 metric tonnes of bronze, which was used for the outer cladding of the structure.

The Sardar Vallabhbhai Patel Rashtriya Ekta Trust (SVPRET), set up by Modi in 2011 arranged some 129 tonnes of iron implements from nearly 100 million farmers in 169,000 villages across all states to construct the base of the statue.

35. In which district of Gujarat, the Statue of Unity is situated?
    (A) Godavari (B) Narmada
    (C) Tapti (D) Kaveri

36. Who has designed the Statue of Unity?
    (A) PM Narendra Modi
    (B) Sardar Vallabh Bhai Patel
    (C) Larsen and Toubro
    (D) Padma Bhushan Ram Vanji Sutar

37. Who constructed Burj Arab and Burj Khalifa?
    (A) Raja Ranjeet Singh
    (B) Padma Bhushan Ram Vanji Sutar
    (C) Larsen and Toubro
    (D) Eversendai

38. Which of the following trust was set up by Narendra Modi?
    (A) The Sardar Vallabhbhai Patel Rastriya Ekta Trust
    (B) Narmada Rastriya Ekta Trust
    (C) Bharat Ekta Trust
    (D) Statue of unity Ekta Trust

39. You are a school head boy, you have been given a task to write a notice about the plastic ban in the school. How would you start the notice after all necessary fields written?
   (A) I need to inform you all that the plastic is banned in the school from tomorrow the date DD/MM/YYYY and so on.
   (B) The principal has told me to inform you all that the plastic is banned in the school from tomorrow the date DD/MM/YYYY and so on.
   (C) This is to inform all the students, teachers and school staff that plastic has been banned in the school premises, with effective from tomorrow, the date DD/MM/YYYY and so on.
   (D) All students, teachers and staff are ordered to not to use the plastic from tomorrow the date DD/MM/YYYY onwards and so on.

Read the following paragraph carefully and mark the correct choice relevant to the following questions.

The web __**auxiliary verb**__ a case of present day innovation that gives a <u>colossal</u> measure of advantages, yet in addition negative reactions. One noteworthy symptom of the web is addiction. Web enslavement is __**adjective**__ among <u>millennials</u>, and these individuals don't understand that they have a compulsion. Being dependent on the web can prompt many reactions which could __**verb**__ your social, enthusiastic, and physical wellbeing.

40. Mark the suitable words to fill in the blank according to the hints.
   (A) was, natural, hide
   (B) has, habitual, relate
   (C) will, beautify, enhance
   (D) is, common or normal, affect or hurt

41. Mark the correct meanings of the underlined words.
   (A) smart, kids (B) black, citizens
   (C) dark, rich (D) huge, new adults.

42. Synonym of web is:
   (A) Internet (B) Social media
   (C) Online sites (D) Computer

43. Choose the best response in every condition.
   Your best friend recently came back from his Disneyland trip. How would he express his experience to you and other friends?
   (A) Poor you. You couldn't visit Disneyland.
   (B) You must have come with me, it's a heaven for kids like me.
   (C) Disneyland is amazing. A place worth being.
   (D) Oh God, I somehow managed in the crowd. But it is impossible for you to manage.

44. You are at a new place and forget your way to your hotel. What would be your reaction to the passing by?
   (A) Excuse me! I think I'm lost. Can you please tell me the way to hotel Mountain View?
   (B) Excuse me! Can you drop me to my hotel?
   (C) Excuse me! Are you lost as I'm?
   (D) You will keep crying until your parents find you.

45. Your friend: Oh no! I've lost my pen again.
   You: ____________
   (A) You will start laughing.
   (B) How forgetful you are!
   (C) Tell me where you saw it last time, I'll help you in finding it.
   (D) How dumb you are!

ACHIEVERS SECTION

46. Choose the best response for the conversation.

Ishika**:** Manu, where's the birthday gift we got for Anisha? I hope we didn't leave it at home, did we?

Manu: ________

Ishika: Let me see in this case... (Remembering) Oh no! Most probably I put it on the sofa while searching for the car keys and left it there only.

Manu: So, we'll head back to home to get it.

(A) You are so forgetful Ishika.
(B) I expected the same from you Ishika.
(C) Why you get the gift. Anisha doesn't want any gift
(D) Well, I thought you kept it in your bag.

47. Change the speech of the sentence.

Ravina said, "What a horrible movie!"

(A) Ravina asked is the movie horrible.
(B) Ravina asked is it a horrible movie.
(C) Ravina exclaimed that it was a horrible movie.
(D) Ravina said that the movie was so horrible.

48. Insert the suitable conjunction.

______ you get involved in your games, show me your report card.

(A) As
(B) After
(C) Before
(D) As soon as

49. Insert the suitable adverb.

I _____ know Himank, how can I ask him to lend me some money?

(A) ever since
(B) personally
(C) hardly
(D) badly

50. What is the meaning of the phrasal verb 'bend over backwards'?

(A) Output hard efforts
(B) Input hard efforts
(C) Never see others back
(D) Knee down your enemies.

Mock Test Paper 2

Total Questions : 50 Time : 1 Hour

I E O

INTERNATIONAL ENGLISH OLYMPIAD

PATTERN AND MARKING SCHEME				
Section	(1) Word and Structure Knowledge	(2) Reading	(3) Spoken and Written Expression	(4)Achievers
No. of Questions		45		5
Marks per Questions		1		3

SYLLABUS

Section – 1 : Synonyms, Antonyms, Analogies and Spellings, Collocations, Phrasal Verbs, Idioms or Proverbs, Homonyms and Homophones, One-Word, Nouns, Pronouns, Verbs, Adverbs, Adjectives, Articles, Prepositions, Prepositional Phrases, Participle Phrases, Conjunctions, Determiners, Jumbled Words and Punctuations, Tenses, Voices and Narrations, Question Tags, etc. Words related to Leisure, Household Items/Issues, Social Causes, Outdoor Locations and Activities, etc.

Section – 2 : Search for and retrieve information from various text types like News Reports, Blurb, Dictionaries, etc., Understand information presented in Instruction Manual Format, Message Format and others. Acquire broad understanding of and look for specific information in longer texts like Editorials, Essays, etc.

Section – 3 : Ability to understand situation-based variations in functions like Requesting, Giving Information, Expressing Surprise, Pronunciation etc.

Section – 4 : Higher Order Thinking Questions - Syllabus as per Sections 1, 2 and 3.

WORD AND STRUCTURE KNOWLEDGE

1. Identify the synonym word for 'Postponed'.
   (A) Continued (B) Fastened
   (C) Adjourned (D) Established
2. Identify the antonym(s) of 'Evolution'.
   (A) devaluation (B) regression
   (C) retrogression (D) all of these
3. Identify the correct word.
   (A) Over- exaggerate
   (B) Exaggerate
   (C) Wider- exaggerate
   (D) Stressed- exaggerate
4. Separate the word which doesn't belong to the group of other words.
   Accommodation, quarters, understanding, comfort, maladaptation, adjustment.
   (A) comfort (B) maladaptation
   (C) adjustment (D) quarters
5. 'Manuscript' stands for ___________.
   (A) A document written by hand rather than printed.
   (B) A document printed on the leaves.
   (C) A document stored in the old computers.
   (D) A document used by our ancestors.
6. What do you understand by the idiom 'crocodile tears'?
   (A) eating without thinking.
   (B) Faking crying
   (C) Crying like crocodile
   (D) False sympathy

7. What does the proverb 'Blessing in disguise' stands for?
(A) Disgusts are blessed.
(B) Mis happenings occurs for good
(C) Bad people are always blessed.
(D) Something that seems bad or unlucky at first, but results in something good happening later.

8. Replace the underlined words with the suitable collective noun.
To fix the engine the mechanic opened his tool box to reach out a number of tools.
(A) a bunch of tools
(B) a set of tools
(C) a flock of tools
(D) a pile of tools

9. Fill in the blank with suitable indefinite pronoun.
_______ among the girls can take part in the dance competition.
(A) anyone (B) none
(C) everyone (D) someone

10. Complete the sentence with suitable auxiliary verbs.
It ______ good that I went to attend the party. The hosts ____ expecting me there.
(A) was, were
(B) is, are
(C) has been, will be
(D) was, will be

11. Replace the underlined word with a suitable phrasal verb.
I am so excited to play a match for our school team tomorrow.
(A) so happy
(B) can't believe
(C) looking forward
(D) not available

12. That leisure feeling when someone draws happiness from something done in accordance to their wish, is called as:
(A) fulfilment (B) satisfaction
(C) free time (D) celebration

13. Identify the set of household items.
(A) sewing machines, refrigerator, spatula
(B) cooking stove, washing machine, can opener
(C) bed sheets, storage container, cabinets
(D) All of these

14. Which of the following comes under social issues?
(A) gender inequality
(B) violence
(C) caste system
(D) all of these

15. Which of the following set represents the category of homophones?
(A) fridge and freeze
(B) frees and fridge
(C) frees and freeze
(D) freeway and freezer

16. What is yard?
(A) homophone (B) homonym
(C) homograph (D) root word

17. Change the underlined adverb into its opposite.
My uncle talks with his staff rudely.
(A) sufficiently (B) politely
(C) affectionately (D) helpfully

18. Choose the most appropriate words which best combines with the adjective 'grinning'.
(A) stars (B) skin
(C) teeth (D) feet

19. Complete the sentence by the insertion of appropriate articles.
We should not leave our friends in their _____ staggered conditions, as ___ best thing of friendship is ___ friend in need is ____ friend indeed.
(A) no article, the, a, a
(B) the, no article, a, an
(C) a, the, a, an
(D) the, the, a, a

20. Insert the suitable preposition.

I am going to visit my parents. I'll stay at my home ____ coming Sunday ____ next Sunday

(A) either, or (B) neither, nor

(C) upon, over (D) from, to

21. Insert the suitable conjunctions.

I've no clue ___ Salil is going for the party __ not.

(A) either, or (B) neither, nor

(C) whether, or (D) none of these

22. Identify the sentence with incorrect use of determiner.

(A) I want to take many pastries from this shop.

(B) The lions are carnivore.

(C) Sameer wants to go his home.

(D) The tree shed its leaves.

23. Arrange the following words into a meaningful sentence.

It/ mandatory/ traffic/ is/ for/ follow/ us/ to/ the rules

(A) mandatory is for us to follow the traffic rules.

(B) to follow the traffic rules is mandatory for us

(C) the traffic rules are mandatory to follow for us

(D) It is mandatory for us to follow the traffic rules.

24. Complete the sentence with correct use of helping verb and verb.

I ______ for you at the platform.

(A) has wait (B) shall wait

(C) shall waiting (D) had waiting

25. Change the voice of the following sentence.

Do it.

(A) Let it be done.

(B) Did it!

(C) Let you be do it.

(D) Let it be done.

26. Change the following direct speech into indirect speech.

Rekha said to Hema, "Will you teach me a dance step?"

(A) Rekha asked Hema if she would teach her a dance step.

(B) Rekha asked Hema whether she would teach her a dance step.

(C) both of these

(D) none of these

27. Insert the appropriate prepositional phrase.

You must have read warning in some hotels or high rise buildings, _______ fire break the glass.

(A) In case of (B) In the case

(C) With case of (D) While the

28. Insert the suitable participle.

_____ is an art, everybody does not know it.

(A) playing (B) sewing

(C) dance (D) song

29. Identify the sentence which is correctly punctuated.

mr sudhir said to me mm son in law is an engineer

(A) Mr. Sudhir said that his son in law is an engineer.

(B) Mr. sudhir said that his son in law; is an engineer.

(C) Mr Sudhir said that; his son-in-law is an engineer!

(D) Mr. Sudhir said to me, "My son-in-law is an engineer."

30. Insert the suitable question tag.

You should follow the rules of the game, ____________

(A) isn't it?

(B) won't you?

(C) shouldn't you?

(D) shall not you

READING

Read the following passage carefully and answer the relevant questions from 31 to 34.

We know that Earth is our planet. It is third planet from Sun after Mercury and Venus. Our galaxy is known as milky way. There are total 8 planets in our solar system. The order of all the planets from Sun is Mercury, Venus, Earth, Mars, Jupiter, Saturn, Uranus, Neptune. Initially Pluto was also considered as the planet 9 in our solar system but later on it was removed from the list because it could not qualify the qualities of a planet. Among all the planet Earth is the only planet which hosts life. Sometimes during night, three brightest planets are visible from the earth, these are Venus, Jupitar and Saturn. Earth is the fifth largest planet after Jupiter, Saturn, Uranus and Neptune. Venus, Mars and Mercury are smaller planets than Earth. Moon is the natural satellite of Earth which revolves around the Earth.

31. What is the name of our galaxy?
    (A) Milky white (B) Milky stars
    (C) Milky way (D) Milky Solar

32. What is the order of Earth in the solar system with respect to the size?
    (A) Third (B) Fourth
    (C) Fifth (D) Sixth

33. What is the place of Earth from Sun?
    (A) Nearest to Sun
    (B) 2nd from the Sun
    (C) 3rd from the Sun
    (D) Farthest from the Sun

34. Which of the following natural satellite of the Earth?
    (A) Moon (B) Jupitar
    (C) Saturn (D) Pluto

Read following poem carefully and answer the question from 35 to 38.

When things go wrong as they sometimes will, When the road you're trudging seems all up hill,

When the funds are low and the debts are high,
And you want to smile, but you have to sigh,

When care is pressing you down a bit, Rest if you must, but don't you quit.

Life is strange with its twists and turns, As every one of us sometimes learns

And many a failure comes about, When he might have won had he stuck it out;

Don't give up though the pace seems slow—
You may succeed with another blow.

Success is failure turned inside out— The silver tint of the clouds of doubt,

And you never can tell just how close you are, It may be near when it seems so far;

So stick to the fight when you're hardest hit— It's when things seem worst that you must not quit.

John Greenleaf Whittier

35. What is the motto of the poet through the poem?
    (A) He is motivating you to not to quit.
    (B) He is letting you down.
    (C) He says that quitting is appropriate.
    (D) Can't be determined.

36. What does you understand by the proverb 'seems all uphill'?
    (A) When you have to move up to a hill.
    (B) It is tough to fulfil any task.
    (C) When everything is situated away from you.
    (D) When accomplishment of everything seems difficult.

37. Why does the poet say that life is strange?
   (A) We can't see our life ourselves.
   (B) Life is full of twists and turns.
   (C) Life is full of failures.
   (D) Life is full of lessons.

38. True explanation of '*Don't give up though the pace seems slow— You may succeed with another blow*' is:
   (A) When our speed is slow, we should not quit, instead we should quit in the next turn.
   (B) We should not quit before the success.
   (C) We should not wait for another chance, we should quit after first failure.
   (D) We should not quit if we don't receive any outcome of the hard work, maybe we get success in the next stroke.

SPOKEN AND WRITTEN EXPRESSIONS

39. Choose the best response from the given options.

   Ekta: Papa, I've been selected as the head girl of the school.

   Father: ___________
   (A) Oh! How come? You are not that intelligent.
   (B) Oh no! Now will behave more rudely.
   (C) Well done! Congratulations my kid.
   (D) I am not happy with this, I want you as the school topper.

40. You want to appreciate a boy of your class for his intelligence. How would you react?
   (A) Oh God! You are so proud of your brain.
   (B) Oh God! You have got a sharp brain, why didn't I?
   (C) Oh! You are intelligent but what about your face?
   (D) Hello! You are really doing good. I want to learn something from you.

41. Suppose you are Eela. You called a restaurant to reserve a seat for you. They confirmed your reservation. What will you say on reaching the place?
   (A) Hi! I am Eela. I have a reservation.
   (B) Hello, I called for the reservation.
   (C) Hello! I'm sure you have saved a seat for me.
   (D) You must have booked a table for me, haven't you?

42. You reside in the outskirts of a metro city and you and other residents have to travel to and fro on daily basis, but there is no bus stop in your area. You want to write a letter to the municipal corporation to set up a bus stop in your area. What would be the subject of your letter?
   (A) Subject: I want a bus stop at Ang Vihar
   (B) Subject: Problems of the residents of Ang Vihar
   (C) Subject: Cause of inconvenience on daily basis.
   (D) Subject: Setting up a bus stop in Ang Vihar.

43. You have to write an informal letter to an unfortunate classmate who recently lost his grandmother. After completing the letter what should be your closing words before your name?
   (A) Yours truly
   (B) With deepest sympathy
   (C) Warm regards
   (D) Thank you for your time

44. Insert suitable punctuation marks.
   he was planning to visit four places agra new delhi mumbai and chennai
   (A) He was planning to visit four places; Agra New Delhi Mumbai and Chennai!
   (B) He was planning to visit four places: Agra, New Delhi, Mumbai and Chennai
   (C) He was planning to visit four places; agra new Delhi mumbai and chennai!
   (D) He was planning, to visit four places: Agra; new Delhi Mumbai and Chennai!

45. Identify the sentence with true future perfect continuous tense.
   (A) Will Ram have delivered his lecture since tomorrow morning?
   (B) Will have Ram being delivered his lecture since morning tomorrow
   (C) Will Ram be delivering his lecture since morning tomorrow?
   (D) None of these

ACHIEVERS SECTION

46. Convert the following sentence into the passive voice.
   Did Manav not open the doors of the main gate?
   (A) Were the doors of main gate not opened by Manav?
   (B) Why did Manav not open the doors of the main gate?
   (C) Why main gate doors were not opened by Manav?
   (D) Were the main gate doors not opened by Manav?

47. Complete the sentence with appropriate tense.
   Grandfather said to children, "Don't make a noise. I _____ trying to sleep for one hour."
   (A) were have been (B) have been
   (C) has been (D) was being

48. Arrange the following jumbled words into a meaningful sentence.
   funds/ agreed/ Bhagat/ cancer/ intentionally/ raise/ patients/ for/ the/ to
   (A) Funds are intentionally raise to cancer patients for the agreed.
   (B) For the agreed cancer patients Bhagat raise to funds intentionally.
   (C) Bhagat intentionally agreed to raise funds for the cancer patients.
   (D) To the funds Bhagat agreed for cancer patients intentionally.

49. Complete the sentence with suitable articles.
   _____honesty is ___ best policy.
   (A) the, the (B) a, the
   (C) a, no article (D) no article, the

50. What is the meaning of idiom 'let bygones be bygones'?
   (A) go with the flow
   (B) don't let your past affect your present
   (C) let's forgive and forget the past quarrels
   (D) don't think about the past

Hints and Solutions

INTERNATIONAL MATHEMATICS OLYMPIAD (IMO)

MOCK TEST PAPER – 1

ANSWERS									
1. (B)	2. (B)	3. (C)	4. (B)	5. (B)	6. (A)	7. (C)	8. (C)	9. (C)	10. (B)
11. (C)	12. (B)	13. (C)	14. (B)	15. (D)	16. (A)	17. (C)	18. (B)	19. (B)	20. (A)
21. (B)	22. (A)	23. (D)	24. (A)	25. (D)	26. (A)	27. (B)	28. (A)	29. (D)	30. (D)
31. (A)	32. (C)	33. (B)	34. (A)	35. (D)	36. (B)	37. (C)	38. (B)	39. (D)	40. (C)
41. (B)	42. (C)	43. (A)	44. (C)	45. (A)	46. (C)	47. (B)	48. (B)	49. (C)	50. (C)

1. (B) Observing the given series, we conclude that 7th term = $7^3 - 7 = 336$. Thus, the term that replace question mark is 336.

2. (B) We have,

Letter	I	N	D	I	A
Code	6	3	5	6	8

3. (C) A is B's father's nephew implies A is the cousin of B. C is also B's cousin, but C is not the brother of A, so C must be the sister of A.

4. (B) Sameera moves from her city at point O to her cousin's city at point A and then to her brother-in-law's city at point B. Clearly, ΔOBA is right-angled triangle at B.

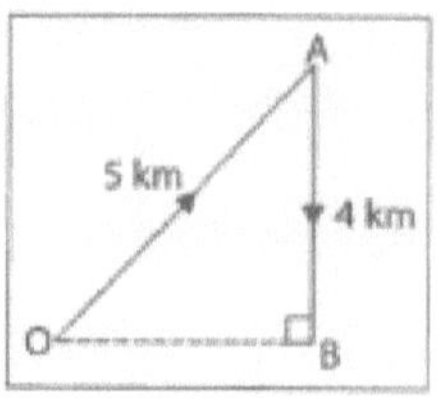

So, $OA^2 = OB^2 + AB^2$

$\Rightarrow OB^2 = OA^2 - AB^2$

$OB = \sqrt{(25-16)\text{km}} = \sqrt{9}\text{ km} = 3\text{ km}$

Sameera is 3 km to the east of her initial position O.

5. (B) The letter common to all the three geometrical figures is Y.

6. (A) Growth of a kid: Infant, Childhood, Puberty, Adolescence, Adulthood.

7. (C) $= 15 \div 3 + 24 - 12 \times 2$

$= 5 + 24 - 24$

$= 5$

8. (C) No. of triangles is 24.

9. (C) The mirror image of the figure (X) is:

10. (B) First figure rotates clock-wise through 90° to become 2nd figure and second one rotates through 180° to become third one. Hence, the correct figure is:

13. (C) The relationship is $x : x^2$, that is, $7 : 7^2$ and $24 : 24^2$

16. (A) Not defined

17. (C) Since, vertex is a point where two or more edges meet, so here (C) is correct option having a vertex.

18. (B) According to question

Sum of all angles at a point

$= 150° + 3x°$

$3x° = 360° - 150°$

$x° = 70°$

No. of candidates from team S = 18

$$60° = \frac{18}{\text{Total candidates}} \times 360°$$

Total candidates = 108

Number of candidates from team R =

$$140° = \frac{\text{Number of candidates from team R}}{108} \times 360°$$

No. of candidates = 42

19. (B) We have,

$3^{m-n} = 27$ and $3^{m+n} = 243$

$m - n = 3$ ...(i)

$m + n = 5$ ...(ii)

On solving both equations, we get $m = 4$

20. (A) Let the no. of ₹ 5 denomination she has $= x$

The no. of ₹ 1 denomination she has $= 160 - 4x$

The no. of ₹ 2 denomination she has $= 3x$

Amount of ₹ 5 denomination $= 5x$

Amount of ₹ 1 denomination $= 160 - 4x$

Amount of ₹ 2 denomination $= 6x$

According to question

$5x + 6x + 160 - 4x = 300$

$7x = 140$

$x = 20$

Hence, the no. of ₹ 5 denominations $= 20$

21. (B)

$$SP = \left[\frac{100-5}{100}\right] \times 500$$

$SP = 475$

$P = 25\%$

$$CP = \left[\frac{100}{125} \times 475\right] = 380$$

22. (A)

$$108° = \frac{(2n-4) \times 90°}{n}$$

$n = 5$

23. (D) Shilpa's age three years ago $= x$

Shilpa's present age $= x + 3$

According to question

Akshita's present age $= 3\,(x + 3)$

24. (A)

$(x+y)^2 = x^2 + y^2 + 2xy$

$(17)^2 = 167 + 2xy$

$2xy = 122$

$xy = 61$

25. (D) If both pipes are opened together

$$= \frac{1}{18} + \frac{1}{12} = \frac{5}{36}$$

Time taken by them to fill the tank

$$= 7\frac{1}{5} \text{ minutes}$$

26. (A) We have,

$$\frac{\sqrt{3}a}{2} = \sqrt{6}$$

$a = 2\sqrt{2}$

$$Area = \frac{\sqrt{3}}{4}a^2$$

$$A = \frac{\sqrt{3}}{4} \times 2\sqrt{2} \times 2\sqrt{2} = 2\sqrt{3} \text{ cm}^2$$

27. (B) Actual distance between the points

$$\frac{8.4}{0.7} \times 4.65 = 55.80 \text{ km}$$

28. (A)

$$2(x+4+3x-2)=60$$
$$4x+2=30$$
$$4x=28$$
$$x=7$$

29. (D)

30. (D) Let the sum be ₹ x

$$420=x\left(1+\frac{10}{100}\right)^2-x$$
$$420=x\left(\frac{11}{10}\right)^2-1$$
$$420=x\left(\frac{121}{100}-1\right)$$
$$420=x\left(\frac{21}{100}\right)$$
$$x=2000$$

SI = ₹ 400

31. (A) We have,

$$V_1=\pi r_1^2 h_1=\pi(3)^2 h_1=\pi 9h_1$$
$$V_2=\pi r_2^2 h_2=\pi(1)^2 h_2=\pi h_2$$
$$V_1=V_2$$
$$\pi 9h_1=\pi h_2$$
$$\frac{h_1}{h_2}=\frac{1}{9}$$

32. (C)

$$\sqrt{248+\sqrt{52+\sqrt{144}}}$$
$$=\sqrt{248+\sqrt{52+12}}$$
$$=\sqrt{248+\sqrt{64}}$$
$$=\sqrt{248+8}$$
$$=\sqrt{256}=16$$

33. (B) Let the no. of men required be x

$$x=\frac{17\times 30}{10}$$
$$x=51$$

No. of extra men = 51 – 30 = 21

34. (A)

$$\left(x^2-y^2\right)$$
$$(x+y)(x-y)$$
$$\left(\sqrt{2}+\frac{1}{\sqrt{2}}\right)\left(\sqrt{2}-\frac{1}{\sqrt{2}}\right)=\frac{3}{2}$$

35. (D) Total possible outcomes is
4 + 6 + 8 = 18

36. (B) We have,
Radius of the circular track = 21 m
Circumference of the circular track

$$=2\pi r=2\times\frac{22}{7}\times 21=132\text{ m}$$

Total distane covered in 30 rounds
= 132 × 30 = 3960 m
His speed on the circular track
= 6 km/h

$$=\frac{6\times 1000}{60}=\frac{1000}{10}=100\text{ m / min}$$

Time taken by him $=\frac{3960}{100}=39.6$ min

Time = 39 min and 36 s

37. (C) Let the number of members in the committee = x
Amount contributed by each member
= ₹ x
According to question

$$x\times x=2209$$
$$x^2=2209$$
$$x=47$$

Hence, the number of members = 47

38. (B) Let the speed of the boat be x km/hr and distance between two ports is y km.
Speed of the stream = 3 km/hr
For downstream:
Speed = $(x + 3)$ km/hr
Time = 3 hr
Distance = $3(x + 3)$ km
For upstream:
Speed = $(x – 3)$ km/hr

Time = 5 hr
Distance = $5(x - 3)$ km
According to question
$3(x + 3) = 5(x - 3)$
$3x + 9 = 5x - 15$
$24 = 2x$
$x = 12$ km/hr
The speed of boat upstream = $(x - 3)$ km/hr = 12 – 3 = 9 km/hr

39. (D) Central angle

$$\frac{40}{100} \times 360 = 144°$$

40. (C) Total balls = x
Blue balls = $x - 104$

$$\text{Probability of blue ball} = \frac{x-104}{x}$$

$$\frac{1}{5} = \frac{x-104}{x}$$

$$x = 5x - 520$$

$$520 = 4x$$

$$x = 130$$

No. of blue balls = 130 – 104 = 26

41. (B) We have,

$$\text{SP of car} - \left[\frac{100+10}{100}\right] \times 300000$$

$$SP = \frac{110}{100} \times 300000$$

$$SP = 330000$$

$$\text{SP of bike} = \left[\frac{100-20}{100}\right] \times 100000$$

$$SP = \frac{80}{100} \times 100000$$

$$SP = 80000$$

Total CP = ₹ 400000
Total SP = ₹ 410000
Net profit = ₹ 10000

$$\text{Profit\%} = \left[\frac{10000}{410000}\right] \times 100$$

$$\text{Profit\%} = 2.5\%$$

42. (C) Let the no. of correct sums = x
Incorrect sums = $(24 - x)$
Marks obtained = 37
According to question

$$3x - 2(24 - x) = 37$$

$$3x - 48 + 2x = 37$$

$$5x = 37 + 48$$

$$5x = 85$$

$$x = 17$$

43. (A) Total cost of air-conditioner = 16000
Profit = 15%

$$SP = \left[\frac{100 + P\%}{100}\right] \times CP$$

$$SP = \frac{115}{100} \times 16000 = 160 \times 115$$

$$= 18400$$

44. (C) Let the no. of days food will last = x days

$$x = \frac{600 \times 140}{500}$$

$$x = 168 \text{ days}$$

45. (A) Distance = speed × Time
Distance = 56 × 4 = 224 km
His new speed = 64 km/h
Distance = 224 km

Time taken to complete the journey with new speed = 224/64 = $3\frac{1}{2}$ hrs

46. (C)

$$y + \cfrac{1}{1 + \cfrac{1}{1 + \cfrac{1}{y}}} = \frac{1}{2} + \cfrac{1}{1 + \cfrac{1}{1 + \cfrac{1}{1/2}}}$$

$$= \frac{1}{2} + \cfrac{1}{1 + \cfrac{1}{1+2}} = \frac{1}{2} + \cfrac{1}{1 + \cfrac{1}{3}}$$

$$= \frac{1}{2} + \frac{1}{4/3} = \frac{1}{2} + \frac{3}{4} = \frac{2+3}{4} = \frac{5}{4}$$

47. (B) Circumference of circle = length of rectangular sheet

$2\pi r = 44$

$r = 7$ cm

Volume of cylinder = $\pi r^2 h$

$= \frac{22}{7} \times 7 \times 7 \times 33 = 5082 \text{ cm}^3$

48. (B) Let Principal be ₹ x

Amount in 4 years = $2x$

$$A = P\left(1 + \frac{r}{100}\right)^n$$

$$2x = x\left(1 + \frac{r}{100}\right)^4$$

$$\left(1 + \frac{r}{100}\right)^4 = 2$$

$$\left(1 + \frac{r}{100}\right) = (2)^{1/4} \text{...(i)}$$

$$A = P\left(1 + \frac{r}{100}\right)^n$$

$$8x = x\left(1 + \frac{r}{100}\right)^n$$

$$\left(1 + \frac{r}{100}\right)^n = 8$$

$$\left(1 + \frac{r}{100}\right) = (2)^{3/n} \qquad \text{...(ii)}$$

From (i) and (ii)

$n = 12$ years

49. (C) $\sqrt{1 + \frac{64}{225}} = 1 + \frac{x}{15}$

$$\sqrt{\frac{289}{225}} = 1 + \frac{x}{15}$$

$$\frac{17}{15} = 1 + \frac{x}{15}$$

$$\frac{x}{15} = \frac{2}{15}$$

$$x = 2$$

50. (C) $3^{\left(\frac{y}{2} - 2\right)} = 9y$

$$3^{\left(\frac{y}{2} - 2\right)} = 3^{2y}$$

$$\frac{y}{2} - 2 = 2y$$

$$\frac{y - 4}{2} = 2y$$

$$y - 4 = 4y$$

$$y = -\frac{4}{3}$$

MOCK TEST PAPER – 2

ANSWERS									
1. (B)	2. (C)	3. (B)	4. (B)	5. (C)	6. (A)	7. (B)	8. (B)	9. (B)	10. (A)
11. (B)	12. (A)	13. (A)	14. (B)	15. (A)	16. (C)	17. (C)	18. (B)	19. (B)	20. (A)
21. (D)	22. (C)	23. (D)	24. (C)	25. (B)	26. (B)	27. (C)	28. (B)	29. (A)	30. (B)
31. (A)	32. (C)	33. (D)	34. (B)	35. (B)	36. (B)	37. (A)	38. (B)	39. (A)	40. (B)
41. (C)	42. (B)	43. (C)	44. (B)	45. (C)	46. (B)	47. (A)	48. (A)	49. (B)	50. (C)

1. (B) $(3 \times 5 \times 2 \times 4) \div 10 = 12$,
$(6 \times 2 \times 3 \times 5) \div 10 = 18$
Similarly $(2 \times 2 \times 5 \times 8) \div 10 = 16$

2. (C) To get second figure, the upper and the lower elements get vertically inverted and combine to form a single element.

3. (B) Birds fly in the sky and sky is star.

4. (B) Daughter of only child of my father means my daughter. So, Sajal's wife is the mother of Aanchal.

5. (C) Let Arya starts from the point P and reach Q.

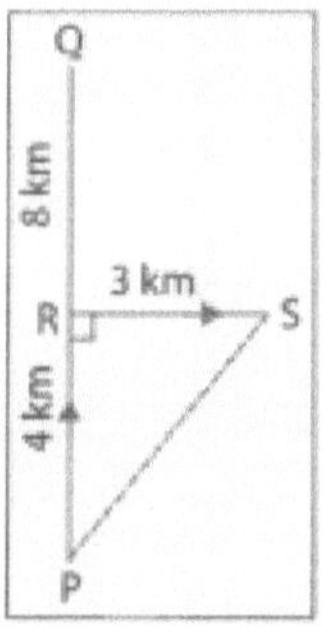

Using Pythagoras theorem, we get
$PS^2 = PR^2 + RS^2 = 4^2 + 3^2 = 25 \Rightarrow$
PS = 5 km
Thus, Arya is 5 km away from the initial point in North-East of the initial point.

6. (A) The letter common to triangle and rectangle only is Q.

7. (B) $52 - 4 \times 5 + 8 \div 2 = 36$

8. (B) After interchanging their positions, Anshul becomes 25th from the right end and 10th from the left end.
So, total number of boys in the row
$= 25 + 10 - 1 = 34$

9. (B) No. of parallelograms is $2 + 2 + 8 + 3 = 15$.

14. (B)

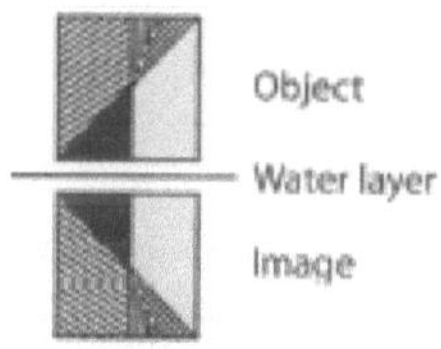

16. (C) The coordinates of Q are (3, 3).

17. (C) Let no. of days food will last = x days

$$x = \frac{300 \times 42}{350} = 36 \text{ days}$$

18. (B) We have,
If $\sqrt{2401} = 49$, then $\sqrt{0.2401}$
$= 0.49$ and $\sqrt{24.01} = 4.9$
$\sqrt{0.2401} + \sqrt{24.01} = 5.39$

19. (B) We have,
Area of trapezium

$$= \frac{1}{2} \times [40 + 20] \times 24 = 720 \text{ cm}^3$$

20. (A) We have

$p^2 - 17p - 38$

$= p^2 - 19p + 2p - 38$

$= p(p - 19) + 2(p - 19)$

$= (p - 19)(p + 2)$

21. (D) Let the sum be x.

$SI = \frac{3x}{10}$

$CI = x\left[1 + \frac{15}{100}\right]^2 - x$

$CI = \frac{129x}{400}$

$CI - SI = 144$

$\frac{129x}{400} - \frac{3x}{10} = 144$

$\frac{129x - 120x}{400} = 144$

$\frac{9x}{400} = 144$

$x = \frac{144 \times 400}{9} = 6400$

22. (C) Length of one of the diagonals is

$d^2 = (10)^2 + (24)^2$

$d^2 = 676$

$d = 26$ cm

23. (D) Let the larger no. be x and smaller no. be y

$\frac{x}{y} = \frac{3}{5}$

$5x = 3y$

$5x - 3y = 0$ ...(i)

$\frac{x - 9}{y - 9} = \frac{12}{23}$

$23x - 207 = 12y - 108$

$23x - 12y = 99$ ...(ii)

On solving (i) and (ii)

$x = 33$

$5x - 3y = 0$

$165 - 3y = 0$

$3y = 165$

$y = 55$

24. (C) We have,

AB = CD (opp. sides of parallelogram)

BC = AD

$2x + 5 = y + 1$

$2x - y = -4$ ....(i)

$3x - 4 = y + 5$

$3x - y = 9$ ...(ii)

On solving (i) and (ii)

$x = 13, \ y = 30$

AB = 31 cm

BC = 35 cm

Ratio of AB : BC = 31 : 35

25. (B) We have,

$2x + 4) = (3x + 1)$

$x = 3$

27. (C) Each interior angle

$= \frac{(2n - 4) \times 90°}{n}$

$135°n = 180°n - 360°$

$n = \frac{360°}{45°} = 8$

28. (B) $100x + 10y + z$

29. (A) We have,

$SP = \left[\frac{100 - 12}{100}\right] \times 1200 = 1056$

30. (B) We have,

$= [(5)^6 \times -(9)^3]^{\frac{1}{3}}$

$= [(5)^2 \times -(9)^1]$

$= 25 \times -9$

$= -225$

31. (A) We have

$$\frac{5x}{3}-4=\frac{2x}{5}$$

$$\frac{5x-12}{3}=\frac{2x}{5}$$

$$25x-60=6x$$

$$19x=60$$

$$x=\frac{60}{19}$$

32. (C) We have

$$N=\sqrt[3]{\sqrt[3]{a^9}}$$

$$N=\sqrt[3]{a^{9\times\frac{1}{3}}}$$

$$N=\sqrt[3]{a^3}$$

$$N=a^{3\times\frac{1}{3}}$$

$$N=a$$

34. (B) $\frac{25}{15}$

35. (B) Probability of selecting 'W' = $\frac{1}{5}$

36. (B) Part of tank filled by both the pipes when opened simultaneously.

$$=\frac{1}{18}+\frac{1}{12}=\frac{2+3}{36}=\frac{5}{36}$$

Time taken = $7\frac{1}{5}$ minutes

37. (A) Total bangles = 20
No. of red bangles = 7

Probability = $\frac{7}{20}$

38. (B) Let the time be x days

$$x=\frac{20\times20}{25}$$

$$x=16$$

39. (A) Circumference of the circle = Length of each side of square sheet

$2\pi r=a$

$$r=\frac{a}{2\pi}$$

$$\therefore \text{ Ratio } =\frac{a}{2\pi}:a=\frac{1}{2\pi}:1=1:2\pi$$

40. (B) By Pythagoras theorem

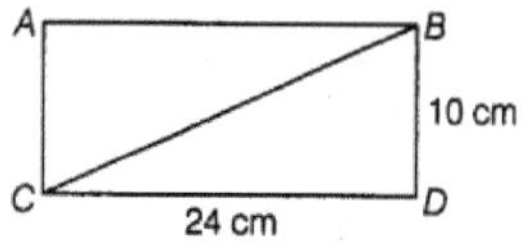

In ΔBCD

$\angle BDC=90°$

We have, $BC^2=BD^2+CD^2$

$\Rightarrow BC^2=10^2+24^2=100+576$

$\Rightarrow BC^2=676$

$\Rightarrow BC=\sqrt{676}$

$\Rightarrow BC=26$ cm

41. (C) Let no. of seats in each row be x
No. of rows = No. of seats in each row $=x$

$x^2=2304$

$x=48$

42. (B) Let no. of students interested in Science $=x$

$$x=\frac{108\times2000}{360}$$

$x=600$

43. (C) Total SP of both the houses = ₹ 751780

CP of one house

$$=\left[\frac{100}{100+15}\right]\times375890$$

$$=\frac{100}{115}\times375890$$

$=326860$

CP of another house

$$=\left[\frac{100}{100-15}\right]\times375890$$

$$=\frac{100}{85}\times375890$$

$=442223$

Total CP = ₹ 76903
Loss = ₹ 17303

$$=\left[\frac{17303}{769083}\right]\times 100$$
$$=2.25\%$$

44. (B) Let the age of Radhika be x and of Kartik be y

According to question

$$\sqrt{x}+\sqrt{y}=7 \quad ...(i)$$
$$\sqrt{x}-\sqrt{y}=1 \quad ...(ii)$$

On solving (i) and (ii)

$x = 16$

Hence, Radhika's age = 16 years

45. (C) Let the weight of bag X = a kg

Y = $3a$ kg

Z = $3a - 4$ kg

Z = 18 – 4 = 14 kg

46. (B) $3x-\frac{1}{3x}=6$, (Given)

On squaring both the sides

$$3x-\frac{1}{3x}=6$$
$$9x^2+\frac{1}{9x^2}-2=36$$
$$9x^2+\frac{1}{9x^2}=38 \quad ...(i)$$

Again on squaring both the sides of (i)

$$9x^2+\frac{1}{9x^2}=38$$
$$81x^4+\frac{1}{81x^4}+2=1444$$
$$81x^4+\frac{1}{81x^4}=1442$$

47. (A) We have,

$$3^y=\frac{\sqrt{3}}{9}$$
$$3^y=\frac{\sqrt{3}}{9}$$
$$3^y=\frac{3^{1/2}}{3^2}$$
$$3^y=3^{1/2-2}$$
$$3^y=3^{-3/2}$$
$$y=-3/2$$

48. (A) We have,

$$\sqrt[3]{\sqrt{0.000064}}$$
$$=\sqrt[3]{0.008}$$
$$=(0.008)^{1/3}$$
$$=(0.02)^{3\times 1/3}$$
$$=0.02$$

49. (B) Let principal be ₹ x

$$\text{S.I.}=\frac{2x}{25}$$
$$\text{C.I.}=\frac{51x}{625}$$
$$\frac{51x}{625}-\frac{2x}{25}=1$$

$x = 625$

Hence, the amount = ₹ 625

50. (C) We have

External Volume

= 120 × 80 × 40 = 384000 cm^3

Internal Volume

= 115 × 75 × 35 = 301875 cm^3

Volume of wood

= 384000 – 301875 = 82125 cm^3

NATIONAL SCIENCE OLYMPIAD (NSO)

MOCK TEST PAPER – 1

ANSWERS									
1. (A)	2. (C)	3. (D)	4. (B)	5. (A)	6. (C)	7. (B)	8. (D)	9. (B)	10. (A)
11. (C)	12. (B)	13. (A)	14. (D)	15. (D)	16. (C)	17. (A)	18. (C)	19. (D)	20. (D)
21. (B)	22. (A)	23. (C)	24. (D)	25. (B)	26. (A)	27. (D)	28. (C)	29. (B)	30. (A)
31. (A)	32. (D)	33. (A)	34. (C)	35. (D)	36. (B)	37. (C)	38. (D)	39. (D)	40. (C)
41. (A)	42. (D)	43. (A)	44. (B)	45. (A)	46. (A)	47. (B)	48. (D)	49. (C)	50. (C)

3. (D)

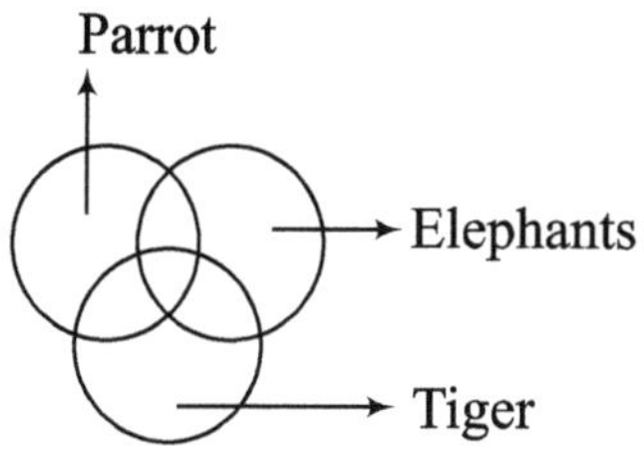

4. (B) As battery has terminals in the same way magnet has poles.

5. (A) All are natural calamities except explosion.

9. (B) Count the number of squares on the basis of following labelling of the squares.

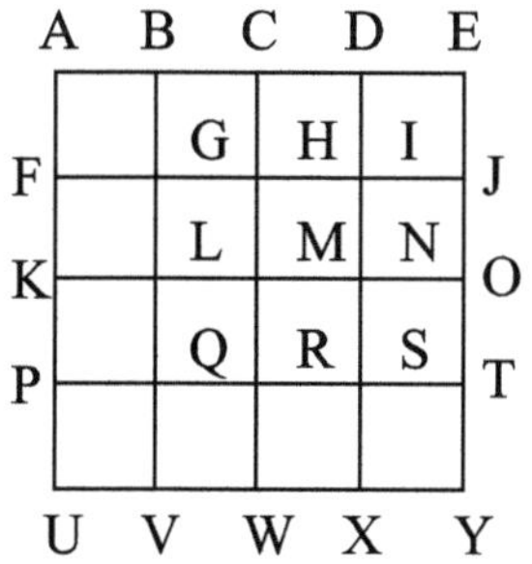

11. (C) Chemical effect is a type of energy, not the force.

12. (B) As we go down in the sea, the pressure increases.

13. (A) A meteor enters the Earth surface with a very high speed. Due to its speed a very high air friction works on it and heat is generated which causes the meteor to burn.

14. (D) Due to friction heat is produced in various parts of the machine. Therefore an amount of heat energy is wasted. As friction opposes motion so noise is produced, and forest fire occurs due to friction between the branches of trees.

15. (D) The disturbance of energy enters in the medium such as air or water and travels along the path of the medium.

16.(C) The speed of sound: In gas (air): 330 – 340 m/s, in liquid (water): 1500 m/s, in solid (steel): 5000 m/s.

17. (A) A substance that dissociates into ions in solution and acquires the capacity to conduct electricity is called as the electrolyte.

20. (D) The charge is written in Coulomb.

21. (B) The glass rod attains positive charge whereas ebonite rod attains negative

charge. Opposite charges attract each other, so both rods will attract each other.

22. (A) Plane-reflecting mirrors are arranged parallelly to each other to target the light directly upto retina.

23. (C) The human eye is a convex lens. The image produced on such lens are real and inverted.

24. (D) Io is the moon of Jupiter.

26. (A) The silk is naturally obtained fibre which has protein in it.

28.(C) Polywool is made up of polyester and wool.

29. (B) Carbon family has 4 electrons, Nitrogen family has 5, Oxygen family has 6 and halogen family has 7 electrons in their outermost shell.

31. (A) Silver chloride is used for the formation of photographic films.

32.(D) Kerosene is less volatile than petrol.

33. (A) High pressure is applied on the gas to liquify it. It is a universal property.

35. (D) Incomplete combustion results into the formation of oxides of nitrogen and carbon which causes air pollution that leads to various respiratory disorders.

37. (C) CO has more oxygen binding affinity than oxygen, therefore it gets bound with RBC and causes lower concentration of oxygen in the blood.

40. (C) Nucleus is the largest organelle of the cell.

42. (D) Microbes have a vast role in the biotechnology.

43. (A) Draught occurs due to rain failure, which leads to the decreased production of the food.

46. (A) As altitude increases, air pressure decreases. The figures in ascending order of heights is sea shore < Triveni Sangam (plain area) < Mountains. Therefore, the correct ascending order of air pressure would be Mountains < Triveni Sangam < Sea Shore

47. (B) When pushing force acts, the object displaces due to motion. Friction works between two surfaces.

49. (C) Milky way is our galaxy and the Sun revolves around the centre of the galaxy.

MOCK TEST PAPER – 2

ANSWERS									
1. (C)	2. (C)	3. (D)	4. (D)	5. (A)	6. (C)	7. (D)	8. (A)	9. (D)	10. (A)
11. (D)	12. (C)	13. (C)	14. (C)	15. (B)	16. (C)	17. (A)	18. (A)	19. (B)	20. (C)
21. (B)	22. (D)	23. (B)	24. (A)	25. (A)	26. (B)	27. (C)	28. (A)	29. (C)	30. (A)
31. (A)	32. (D)	33. (C)	34. (A)	35. (B)	36. (C)	37. (D)	38. (D)	39. (D)	40. (B)
41. (C)	42. (C)	43. (B)	44. (D)	45. (A)	46. (A)	47. (C)	48. (B)	49. (B)	50. (B)

2. (C) Except option C all are made of three lines segment.

6. (C) She is in the North with respect to her house.

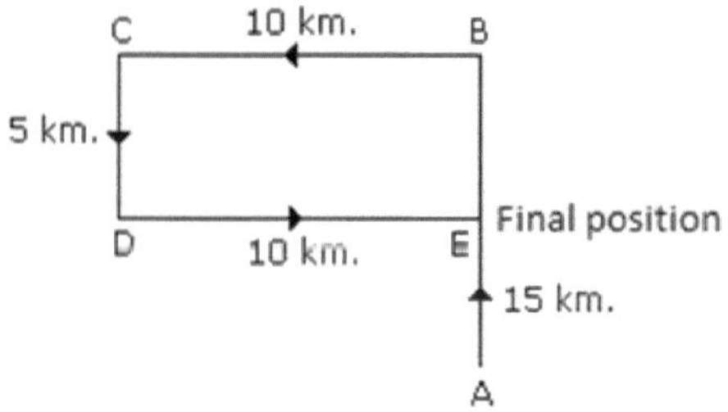

7. (D)

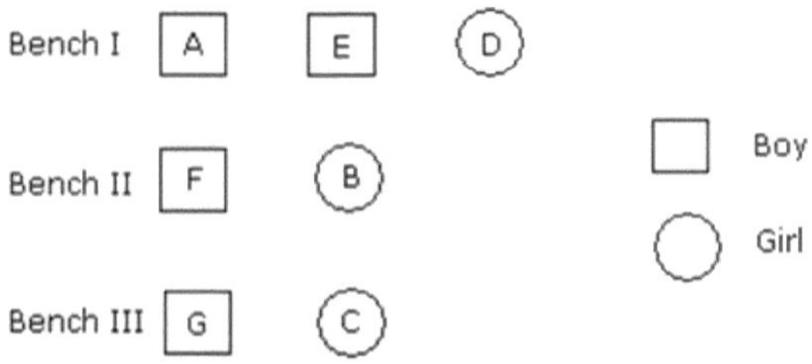

9. (D) As given in the question ages of B = D.
A = B+3 and A = C–3
Thus, B+3 = C–3 ↔ D+3 = C–3 ↔ C–D = 6

10. (A)

$$A_2 \xrightarrow{+2} C_4 \xrightarrow{+2} E_6$$

$$M_5 \xrightarrow{+2} O_9 \xrightarrow{+2} Q_{14}$$

$$G_3 \xrightarrow{+2} I_5 \xrightarrow{+2} K_8$$

13. (C) Flow of energy is unidirectional, it flows from the lowest trophic level to highest trophic level.

14. (C) Bacteriophages kills bacteria.

17. (A) Winnowing involves usage of wind to remove the chaff of the grain.

19. (B) Combustion of fuels like coal in power plants is the main source of sulphur dioxide emissions.

20.(C) Petrol contains lead in a big amount, so burning of petrol causes release of lead into the air.

21. (B) Carbon dioxide is a green house gas as it traps the heat within the atmosphere. If CO_2 is removed, then the temperature will reduce.

24. (A) 400-500 °C is applied during fractional distillation for the separation of the impurities.

25. (A) The vapour pressure of the vapours produced at highest boiling point is very low, so they cannot reach upto the highest point and get condensed at the lower portion of the fractional column.

27. (C) Sulphur is used for the hardening of the rubber.

28.(A) The correct order of reactivity is as following

Na> Ca > Mg> Al > Zn > Fe > Sn > Pb >Cu > Hg > Ag > Au > Pt

29. (C) Polymerization of ethylene results into the formation of polythene.

30. (A) Thermoplastics are bad conductors of heat and electricity.

31. (A) Petrochemicals are obtained from natural gas and petroleum.

34. (A) The plane mirror shows the lateral inversion.

35. (B) Geographical conditions of Japan causes most of the earthquakes.

36. (C) The static electricity discharge produces spark.

37. (D) As the name suggests, nichrome is the alloy of nickel and chromium. It is the only alloy of these two metals.

39. (D) Electrolyte solutions dissociate into positive and negative charges and the ions carry the charge.

40. (B) Frequency = 1/time period. = 1/unit of time = sec-1

41. (C) The larger the amplitude, the louder is the sound produced.

43. (B) Friction can never be zero.

45. (A) The force of the ball changes the position of the pins and the balls fall down.

46. (A) Higher the pitch, greater is the frequency of the sound. Characteristic feature of sound is the pitch, and it is dependent on the frequency of sound.

47. (C) LEDs are more expensive than bulb.

48. (B) The angle between reflected ray and incident ray = $\angle i + \angle r$

According to the given figure,

$i = 90° - 25° = 65°$

As we know $\angle i = \angle r$

So, $\angle i + \angle r = 65° + 65° = 130°$

50. (B) Green revolution is dependent on the weedicides, pesticides, and fertilizers, which are eventually harmful for the soil.

NATIONAL CYBER OLYMPIAD (NCO)

MOCK TEST PAPER – 1

ANSWERS

1. (B)	2. (C)	3. (A)	4. (D)	5. (C)	6. (B)	7. (A)	8. (C)	9. (B)	10. (C)
11. (C)	12. (A)	13. (D)	14. (D)	15. (B)	16. (A)	17. (C)	18. (B)	19. (D)	20. (B)
21. (A)	22. (D)	23. (C)	24. (B)	25. (A)	26. (D)	27. (B)	28. (C)	29. (A)	30. (D)
31. (B)	32. (C)	33. (A)	34. (C)	35. (B)	36. (D)	37. (C)	38. (A)	39(B)	40. (C)
41. (D)	42. (A)	43. (B)	44. (D)	45. (C)	46. (A)	47. (C)	48. (B)	49. (C)	50. (D)

2. (C) In the given analogy, first letter is replaced by third, third is replaced by fifth, fourth is replaced by first and fifth is replaced by fourth.

3. (A) Keyboard is Desk. So, Desk is useful to type.

4. (D) Umang is maternal uncle of the child as the child is daughter of his sister.

5. (C) and the direction is North-east.

6. (B) The minimum number of straight lines required to make the given figure is 8.

7. (A) Some Chairs are made from wood and some are from plastic and other material and cup is not made up of wood. So, diagram (A) represents the best relation between wood, chair and cup.

9. (B) Figure in option (B) is similar to the folded form of the given sheet.

10. (C) In the given figure, the dot is present in the region common to the triangle and square only.

11. (C) MS Excel is a spreadsheet application.

12. (A) ROM is a type of memory that is used to store BIOS instructions, embedded in the computer motherboard.

13. (D) To define the title of a work in HTML, <cite> tag is used.

14. (D) <ul> is used to create an unordered list.

15. (B) Lasso tool is used to select an object in free form.

16. (A) Feature shown in option (A) is used to find the similar meaning of a word.

17. (C) Alt+Ctrl+M is used to insert a new comment in a document.

18. (B) The given feature of MS PowerPoint is used to adjust the spacing between the characters.

19. (D) The feature given in option (D) is used to hide a slide form the presentation.

20. (B) Insert key cannot be used to go to the next or previous slide in slide show view.

21. (A) Plug and play peripherals allows users to connect a device to a computer.

22. (D) Central Processing unit is a hardware.

23. (C) SRAM is a volatile type of memory.

24. (B) Random access memory is the place where the data in current use is stored.

25. (A) hspace attribute of <img> tag adds space to the left and right side of an

image.

26. (D) The given tool is called as Free transform tool.
27. (B) Ctrl+F4 is keystroke that is used to close an active window.
28. (C) The given feature of MS word converts the selected text into a hyperlink.
29. (A) The sum of cells A1 through A59 is the output of =SUM(A1:A59).
30. (D) The AutoSum function displays the sum of selected cells in MS Excel.
31. (B) =TODAY() in MS Excel is used to enter current date.
32. (C) In MS access, rows are called as records.
33. (A) In MS Access, Home tab→Sort & Filter Group→Filter is used to access filter feature.
34. (C) The given feature of MS Access launches the query wizard in MS Access.
35. (B) Static web page is delivered directly to the user exactly as stored.
36. (D) Google, DuckDuckGo and Yahoo are the search engines but Opera mini is a web browser.
37. (C) Amazon is a shopping site and it cannot be used to communicate with friends.
38. (A) Topology shown in option (A) represents Tree topology.
39. (B) Ethernet network is also known as Wired network.
40. (C) The full form of OSI is Open system Interconnection.
41. (D) Google Wallet allows users to send and receive money from mobile devices.
42. (A) Proximity sensor in mobile phones are used to detect the presence of nearby objects without any physical contacts.
43. (B) Multi-tasking operating system allows a user to perform more than one task at the same time.
44. (D) Firewall is not a threat for electronic payment system because firewall used to protect the computer from hacking.
45. (C) Firewall security is used to prevent all unauthorized access to your computer.
46. (A) OMR is a technique which is used for input text into a computer by means of a document reader.
47. (C) Hard disc is a non-volatile and non-sequential access memory device.
48. (B) Compare feature of MS word compares two versions of a document.
49. (C) The feature shown in the figure allows checks the presentation for content that people with disabilities might find difficult to read.
50. (D) a-(iii), b-(iv), c-(ii), d-(i)

MOCK TEST PAPER – 2

ANSWERS									
1. (A)	2. (D)	3. (C)	4. (B)	5. (C)	6. (A)	7. (B)	8. (D)	9. (B)	10. (A)
11. (B)	12. (C)	13. (A)	14. (D)	15. (B)	16. (C)	17. (B)	18. (A)	19. (A)	20. (C)
21. (B)	22. (D)	23. (C)	24. (A)	25. (D)	26. (B)	27. (C)	28. (A)	29. (D)	30. (A)
31. (B)	32. (B)	33. (D)	34. (A)	35. (C)	36. (B)	37. (C)	38. (D)	39. (A)	40. (D)
41. (B)	42. (C)	43. (A)	44. (C)	45. (B)	46. (A)	47. (A)	48. (C)	49. (B)	50. (C)

1. (A) In this series, a random number 13 is interpolated every third number into a simple addition series in which each number is increased by 4.

2. (D) Each corresponding letter is replaced by 6th letter in increasing order of English alphabet.

3. (C) In this coding system, first letter of each word is replaced by 4th letter next to it, second letter is replaced by 5th letter next to it, third letter is replaced by 6th letter next to it and fourth letter is replaced by 7th letter next to it.

4. (B) R and S are the daughters of Q and P is the brother of Q. So, P is the maternal uncle of S.

5. (C) Raj is standing in North-East direction of Rohit.

6. (A) There are 28 triangles in the given figure.

7. (B) There are 25 boys in the row.

8. (D) Figure in option (D) is the water image of the given combination of letters and numbers.

9. (B) Figure (X) is a part of figure (1).

10. (A) The numbers adjacent to four dots are 1 and 5. By rotating the dice, it can be found that there are dots on face opposite to the face containing four dots.

11. (B) Machine language is directly understood by the computer without any conversion.

13. (A) <hr> tag is used to put a horizontal line in HTML.

14. (D) Bgcolor is an attribute of <body> tag that is used to specify the background color of the document.

15. (B) Ctrl+F8 is used to create a new symbol.

16. (C) 'Display of Review' can be accessed by going to Review tab→ Tracking group.

17. (B) Insert tab→Links group Bookmark' is used to open bookmark window.

18. (A) Presenter View is used to display a presentation on two monitors.

19. (A) Slide Show tab→Set Up→Group→-Show Media Controls can be used to show play controls during the slide show.

20. (C) The given feature of MS PowerPoint is used to create a full-fidelity video from the current presentation via web or e-mail.

21. (B) Firmware is a software that is used by the products like remote control,

digital watches and microwave ovens.

22. (D) Projector is an output device that is used for presentation or for viewing videos.
23. (C) NVRAM stands for Non-volatile random-access memory.
24. (A) SD card is a non-volatile memory card that is used in portable devices such as tablets and mobile phones.
25. (D) <li> and </li> in HTML is used to display the items in bulleted form.
26. (B) Onion skin allows a user to view several frames when creating animations in Adobe flash CS6.
27. (C) Hand tool is used to move the stage in all direction without changing the magnification.
28. (A) In MS word, Ctrl+Shift+P is used to change the font size.
29. (D) The formula is trying to multiply a value is not a cause of the NULL error.
30. (A) The given feature is Name Manager and it is used to create, edit and delete names used in the workbook.
31. (B) COUNTUP is an invalid function.
32. (B) Queries in MS Access is used to view, change and analyse the data in different ways.
33. (D) In MS Access, manage replies can be accessed by 'External Tab→Collect data→Manage Replies'.
34. (A) Symbol shows in option (A) represents Design View in MS Access.
35. (C) HTML stands for Hypertext Markup language.
36. (B) Web 3.0 is also known as the semantic web.
37. (C) To erase cookies from the PC, delete temporary internet files.
38. (D) Router is a device that forwards data packets between computer networks.
39. (A) The full form of FMTP is File Multicast Transport Protocol.
40. (D) In Ring network topology, each node is connected to exactly two other nodes to form a single continuous pathway for signals through each node.
41. (B) The given symbol represents the Twitter.
42. (C) Smart covers in tablet computers protect the touchscreen and save energy.
43. (A) Apart from google which is a search engine, Apple macOS, Microsoft Windows and Apple iOS are operating systems.
44. (C) Key logger is a spyware.
45. (B) The first virus of the computer is known as Creeper.
46. (A) The device shown is printer which is an output device. It accepts text and graphic output from a computer and transfer the information to the paper.
47. (A) Cache memory is a temporary memory that keeps certain data available for quick references.
48. (C) Recent Pane of file tab is a feature in MS word that helps you to recover unsaved documents.
49. (B) a-(iv), b-(i), c-(ii), d-(iii)
50. (C) The correct formula will be =A2*0.18

INTERNATIONAL ENGLISH OLYMPIAD (IEO)

MOCK TEST PAPER – 1

ANSWERS									
1. (B)	2. (A)	3. (A)	4. (B)	5. (D)	6. (C)	7. (B)	8. (A)	9. (D)	10. (B)
11. (C)	12. (A)	13. (D)	14. (C)	15. (B)	16. (A)	17. (D)	18. (C)	19. (D)	20. (A)
21. (C)	22. (B)	23. (B)	24. (D)	25. (A)	26. (C)	27. (B)	28. (D)	29. (C)	30. (D)
31. (A)	32. (A)	33. (B)	34. (C)	35. (B)	36. (D)	37. (D)	38. (A)	39. (C)	40. (D)
41. (D)	42. (A)	43. (C)	44. (A)	45. (C)	46. (D)	47. (C)	48. (C)	49. (C)	50. (B)

3. (A) A word formed from the verb is called as the participle, mostly by adding -ing or -ed.

5. (D) When we greet someone good night, good morning, good afternoon or good bye, it gets converted into bid.

9. (D) Determiners are the words which are placed to introduce the noun.

15. (B) homonyms are two words with same spelling and pronunciation while different meaning. Second stands for the unit of time and an order following to first.

16. (A) cymbal is a music instrument and symbol is a recognising mark. Homophones have same pronunciation but different meaning and spelling.

17. (D) Taj Mahal is one of the seven wonders of the world. Foreign tourists visit India primarily to visit Taj Mahal.

19. (D) The activity which involves some risk is called as an adventure.

24. (D) To kill two birds with one stone literally means, performing two tasks at the same moment.

25. (A) In the mythology of some other country cats are associated with storms and dogs are associated with winds. Idioms are the group of words, which are used to make someone understand the real situation.

27. (B) Soothing and convenient can be considered as the antonyms of difficult. Rest are synonyms of difficult.

29. (C) Melodious refers to the sweet sound.

36. (D) Statue of unity is the statue of Sardar Vallabh Bhai Patel, it was inaugurated by PM Narendra Modi. Padma Bhushan Ram Van Ji Sutar has designed the statue while Larsen and Toubro built it.

50. (B) Bend over backwards is a motivational phrasal verb to motivate people to work hardest in order to achieve their desired success.

MOCK TEST PAPER – 2

ANSWERS									
1. (C)	2. (D)	3. (B)	4. (B)	5. (A)	6. (B)	7. (D)	8. (B)	9. (A)	10. (A)
11. (C)	12. (B)	13. (D)	14. (D)	15. (C)	16. (B)	17. (B)	18. (C)	19. (A)	20. (D)
21. (C)	22. (B)	23. (D)	24. (B)	25. (D)	26. (C)	27. (A)	28. (B)	29. (D)	30. (C)
31. (C)	32. (C)	33. (C)	34. (A)	35. (A)	36. (D)	37. (B)	38. (D)	39. (C)	40. (D)
41. (A)	42. (D)	43. (B)	44. (B)	45. (C)	46. (A)	47. (B)	48. (C)	49. (D)	50. (C)

1. (C) You must have heard in the movies 'the court has adjourned for tomorrow.'

2. (D) Evolution refers to the growth, development of the society, diversity or anything.

3. (B) The term exaggerate already stands for the situation of over stressed. Adding other prepositions or adverbs with exaggerate comes under grammatical mistake.

4. (B) Except maladaptation, rest all words are synonyms of each other.

6. (B) Idioms are the group of words which impose a meaning other than the actual meaning of the words.

13. (D) All the items which are useful for the household activities and are easily available at home are called as household item. Watch out for all the substances around you.

14. (D) All the issues which affect the social health comes under social issues.

15. (C) Homophones are two words with same pronunciation but different spelling and meaning.

16. (B) Homonyms are two words with same spelling and pronunciation but different spelling. Yard stands for the ground around a building as well as yard is a unit of length.

22. (B) Determiners are of four types, article is one of them. Determiners are not used in front of plural noun. Determiners are placed before the singular noun.

26. (C) In interrogative type of speech, the speech can be changed into two forms. Question mark is not placed at the end of the sentence.

27. (A) Prepositional phrases contain prepositions and lack verb and adjectives.

28. (B) Participle are the words derived from a verb. In this case participle is serving as the noun.

32. (C) Jupiter, Saturn, Uranus and Neptune are larger than Earth.

33. (C) Mercury is closest to Sun followed by Venus.

35. (A) It is motivational poem.

37. (B) Twists and turns of life refer to the unexpected situations we face in our life. As we are not familiar to those situations, therefore the poet stated that life is strange.

44. (B) Colon (:) is used to introduce a series.

45. (C) Future perfect continuous is used for the actions which will start at a certain time in future and will last at certain time in future. For interrogative sentence the template of the sentence is Shall/ will + Subject + have been + verb's first form + ing.

9 789357 942331

Printed by Libri Plureos GmbH in Hamburg,
Germany